Connecting Arithmetic to Algebra

Strategies for Building Algebraic Thinking in the Elementary Grades

Susan Jo Russell, Deborah Schifter, and Virginia Bastable

TERC

HEINEMANN
Portsmouth, NH

Heinemann
361 Hanover Street
Portsmouth, NH 03801–3912
www.heinemann.com

Offices and agents throughout the world

 This material is based on work supported in part by the National Science Foundation under Grant No. ESI-0550176. Any opinions, findings, and conclusions or recommendations expressed in this material are those of the authors and do not necessarily reflect the views of the National Science Foundation.

Library of Congress Cataloging-in-Publication Data
Russell, Susan Jo.
    Connecting arithmetic to algebra : strategies for building algebraic thinking in the elementary grades/ Susan Jo Russell, Deborah Schifter, Virginia Bastable.
        p. cm.
    Includes bibliographical references and index.
    ISBN-13: 978-0-325-04191-9
    ISBN-10: 0-325-04191-1
    1. Algebra—Study and teaching (Elementary). 2. Problem solving in children.
3. Critical thinking in children. I. Schifter, Deborah. II. Bastable, Virginia. III. Title.
    QA159.R87 2011
    372.7—dc23   2011022813

Editor: *Katherine Bryant*
Production editor: *Sonja S. Chapman*
Typesetter: *Shawn Girsberger*
Interior design: *Shawn Girsberger*
Cover design: *Monica Crigler*
Manufacturing: *Steve Bernier*

Printed in the United States of America on acid-free paper
15   14   13   12   VP   2   3   4   5

CONTENTS

PREFACE

· · · · · · · · · · · ·

$$9 + 6 = 10 + 5 \qquad 35 + 47 = 32 + 50 \qquad 197 + 458 = 200 + 455$$

What is going on in these three equations?

D o you see any commonality in how the expression on the left in each equation is related to the expression on the right? Is there a general idea about addition for which all of these equations could be examples?

Connecting Arithmetic to Algebra is a resource to help teachers deepen their students' understanding of number and operations while preparing them for later instruction in algebra. It introduces ideas that support the learning of *all* students, including students who have a history of difficulty in grade-level computation and students who have generally been successful.

The study of number and operations is core content in the elementary grades. In this book, we present the experiences of elementary teachers who integrate a focus on the properties and behaviors of operations into this core content. This approach is not additional content but a way of thinking about arithmetic that strengthens students' understanding and will serve them well in developing fluent computation and in their transition to formal algebra in later grades. A focus on the operations emphasizes noticing, describing, representing, and explaining consistencies across many problems. Generalizing in this way about the properties and behaviors of the operations is not about solving particular problems but about regularities that are foundational to arithmetic and algebra.

The book is a product of research, classroom inquiry, and mathematical analyses that respond to concerns about algebra's role in enabling students to go further in mathematics. In the early 1990s, a great deal of publicity was given to the way in which secondary algebra courses act as filters; it was asserted that students who took and passed algebra courses had many more educational and professional opportunities open to them than those who did not. One response to this concern was a movement to require that all students take ninth-grade algebra and, in some districts, take it earlier, in eighth or even seventh grade. But in the past, many students who were enrolled in algebra did not pass it; there would be no point in enrolling more students only to have them fail. The natural question arises: What can happen in the elementary grades to better prepare students for algebra?

The authors of *Connecting Arithmetic to Algebra* are among several teams in the country that took on this question. We present in this book our findings that students can be better prepared for algebra *by learning the content of elementary school arithmetic more deeply*. We show how elementary teachers shape their arithmetic instruction so that students learn to investigate the behavior of the operations. Students in these classrooms develop representations for the actions of the operations and think through contexts to which the operations apply. They notice and articulate commonalities across problems, and they prove or disprove generalizations, explaining *why* such generalizations must be or cannot be true. In this way, students become familiar with general rules that underlie the computation strategies they use in arithmetic and that also form the basis of strategies and manipulations they will encounter in later years in algebra courses.

The classroom work on which this book is based took place in 2006 to 2009, as part of a project supported by a National Science Foundation grant. In this project, we collaborated closely with a small group of teachers. At our meetings, teachers took on mathematical challenges for themselves that involved noticing, articulating, and proving generalizations. For example, they considered whether equations like those at the beginning of this preface illustrate a general rule. The teachers noticed that the claim they eventually articulated—if you subtract some amount from one addend and add the same amount to the other, the total remains the same—is also an observation their students frequently make. Even if students do not state the idea explicitly, it may be implicit as they solve addition problems. The teachers began to work from a new perspective: What can we learn about the operations by explicitly investigating, articulating, and representing such general claims?

The teachers began to investigate their students' thinking about such generalizations. They posed problems that brought their students into these ideas and recorded the classroom interactions that ensued. Throughout the project, they transcribed passages of classroom discussion they considered significant in terms of students' learning and their own teaching, and wrote narratives based on the transcriptions. Many of these narratives have been incorporated into this book.

We (teachers and project staff) came to see that structuring lessons to elicit students' ideas encourages students to notice generalizations about addition, subtraction, multiplication, and division. Furthermore, we found that investigating such generalizations takes students into the heart of their study of number and operations. At a meeting toward the end of the project, the teachers explained that they used to think of the focus of the K–5 arithmetic curriculum as understanding numbers and learning to compute efficiently. Now they had identified a third objective of equal weight—investigating the behavior of the operations.

Connecting Arithmetic to Algebra begins with two chapters that introduce generalization in the context of arithmetic and why it is an important part of instruction in the elementary grades. The first chapter describes how teachers can begin to notice when students' work is based on implicit generalizations, and the second offers strategies to help bring implicit generalizations to the surface.

Through our work with teachers, we have learned that discussion focused on the behavior of the operations supports the learning of a range of students, including both those who have difficulty in grade-level computation and those who show a great deal of competence in it. Chapter 3 describes a wide range of students participating in productive discussion about the operations.

The next chapters elaborate on different components of working with students on generalizing about the behavior of the operations: articulating general claims (Chapter 4) and proving general claims (Chapter 5).

After these chapters about content-centered instructional issues, we return to the topic of the range of learners in Chapter 6, presenting individual students with different learning needs and illustrating how their teachers support them to build their knowledge of the operations.

The following two chapters continue with the mathematics of general claims. Chapter 7 discusses the use of arithmetic and algebraic notation in the elementary grades. Chapter 8 returns to the topic of proof, with a focus on how students think through to what numbers their claims apply and a look at how some students incorporate symbolic notation into their work.

Chapter 9 examines how understanding the behavior of the operations supports students' study of mathematics in middle school. Finally, Chapter 10 illustrates how, across the school year, students and teachers develop a community in which a focus on generalizing in the context of arithmetic gradually becomes an expected part of everyday mathematics instruction.

Connecting Arithmetic to Algebra is written for teachers who want their students to deepen their understanding through investigating the behavior of the operations. You may want to form a study group to read the book together with colleagues and discuss what you are reading; the questions at the end of each chapter can help you structure these discussions. Teachers using this book find they need to investigate the mathematics content for themselves, working through the problems presented to students in the classroom episodes and thinking through their own and students' representations. As you bring these ideas to your students, you may find it valuable, as our project teachers did, to document what happens: write up a passage of classroom dialogue, detailing what your students say and do, to reflect on with colleagues.

Although this book can be read by individuals or study groups, it was also designed to be the text for a school-year-long course, which has been given in both online and face-to-face settings. In 2009–10, we assessed grades 2–5 students in classrooms of teachers who took the online course. Students in all grades improved significantly in content related to the course, particularly in determining whether two expressions are equal or an equation is true. For example, students were able to explain why $9 - 5$ is equivalent to $10 - 6$ but not equivalent to $5 - 9$; and that 6×7 is equivalent to 3×14 but not to 5×8. They were better able to determine the missing number in a equation such as $36 + 11 = 26 + \underline{\quad}$ by reasoning that because 26 is 10 less than 36, the missing number must be 10 more than 11. In fact, on the posttest, younger students successfully solved more problems than the older students did on their pretest.

In this course, participants read the first chapters at the beginning of the school year when they can initiate a new set of routines; they read the final chapters in the spring when they can reflect on the progress they have made with their students. When we have taught the course, we divided the work into three large chunks: Chapters 1–4 from September to November, Chapters 5–7 from January to February, and Chapters 8–10 from March to May. The *Connecting Arithmetic to Algebra Course Guide* is a downloadable guide that provides more details about how to structure the course for either an online or face-to-face setting, including suggested mathematics activities, writing assignments, and slides to use for online webinars that are part of the course. The Course Guide will be available for purchase at www.heinemann.com beginning in January 2012.

This book is the product of contributions from many individuals. We thank our colleagues in mathematics and mathematics education who reviewed a draft of this book and gave us important constructive feedback: William S. Bush, Thomas P. Carpenter, Linda Davenport, Ben Ford, W. James (Jim) Lewis, Amy Morse, Virginia Stimpson, and Mary Jo Tavormina. We also thank our colleagues in the Professional Development Study Group who gave us feedback on early versions of individual chapters and Megan Franke for her always insightful comments as our work progressed.

Most especially, we are indebted to the teachers (listed on the following page) who worked closely with us for three years, coming to each project meeting open to learn and willing to share their thinking when they were muddled, when they were clear, and when they were just coming to new insights. These teachers thoughtfully incorporated nascent ideas into their practice, investigated their students' thinking, and diligently wrote about their students and their teaching practice so that we could all learn from their reflections. Now these teachers speak directly to readers of this book through their classroom stories. We invite you to share in what we have learned through this collaborative work.

Susan Jo Russell
Deborah Schifter
Virginia Bastable

January 2011

COLLABORATING
TEACHERS

Tim Baldwin

Leah Blake

Jan Busey

Amy Callen

Holly Concannon

Nikki Costello

Maureen Dillow

Nikki Faria-Mitchell

Christopher Fraley

Marta Garcia

Scott Hendrickson

Leslie Kramer

John MacDougall

Ezinwa Nwankwo

Nonye Obiora

Nadine O'Garro

Anne Marie O'Reilly

Laura Podraza

Cara Pollard

Lara Ramsey

Karen Schweitzer

Bert Speelpenning

Pam Szczesny

Jan Szymaszek

Betsy Thurlow

Ana Vaisenstein

Polly Wagner

1

• • • • • •

Generalizing in Arithmetic
Getting Started, Part I—Noticing

In a second-grade class, students list expressions equal to 15. After students come up with a number of expressions, such as 7 + 8, 5 + 5 + 5, and 20 − 5, the teacher, Louise Craig, adds a constraint:

Ms. Craig: Here's a trickier one. I'd like you to come up with a number sentence that equals 15 and includes a zero.

Corey: 15 minus zero.

Ms. Craig: How do you know?

Corey: If you minus nothing, you can't minus anything . . . if you take nothing away the number is the same.

Eduardo: 15 PLUS zero. It's the same thing, but opposite.

The students in this classroom are engaged in a familiar arithmetic activity—generating expressions equivalent to a particular number. But when the teacher asks Corey how she knows that 15 − 0 equals 15, Corey makes a general statement about subtracting zero: when you subtract zero, *"the number* is the same.*"* Notice Corey is not specifying 15, but talking about "the number" as if to say she could start with any number, subtract zero, and end up with the same number.

This book examines how instruction in computation can be enriched and deepened by a focus on generalizing about the four basic operations—addition, subtraction, multiplication, and division. It provides examples of how teachers in grades 1–6 can incorporate such a focus into their mathematics instruction to strengthen all students' fluency with and understanding of the basic operations. Included are accounts of how both students who excel and students who struggle with grade-level computation can benefit from this work.

GENERALIZING ABOUT THE OPERATIONS— A FOUNDATION OF ARITHMETIC

Children spend much time in mathematics solving individual problems. But the core of the discipline of mathematics is looking *across* multiple examples to find patterns, notice underlying structure, form conjectures about mathematical relationships, and, eventually, articulate and prove general statements. Once Corey has brought up the idea that subtracting zero from any number results in that same number, the class has an opportunity to work on this idea explicitly. Corey's idea is not about the number zero, but about how zero behaves *as part of a particular arithmetic operation.* Corey and Eduardo are identifying an important property of addition and subtraction. Later Deirdre comments, "I think times zero is the same thing." As the class continues this discussion, they will find that adding zero to or subtracting zero from a number results in that number, but multiplying a number by zero does not. Deirdre's conjecture is incorrect, but her idea allows the class to notice how addition and subtraction differ from multiplication.

These second graders are on a journey to understanding the foundations of arithmetic—how the operations behave, what their properties are, and how they are related to each other. These students are starting to think about the general ideas underlying arithmetic.

We study mathematics, in part, so that we can solve problems in daily life. But mathematics is also a way of thinking that involves studying patterns, making conjectures, looking for underlying structure and regularity, identifying and describing relationships, and developing mathematical arguments to show when and why these relationships hold. We use ideas about such mathematical relationships to solve problems, often without noticing. For example, suppose you are standing in a store, figuring out your change from a $10 bill for two items you are buying. One costs $2.49 and one costs $4.99. (Pause here for a moment before reading on and think through how you would solve this problem mentally.)

One method you might use is: $2.49 is almost $2.50, and $4.99 is almost $5.00. $5.00 plus $2.50 is $7.50. If the cost were actually $7.50, the change from your $10.00 would be $2.50, but you added $.02 to the sum of the actual prices. Your actual cost is

2¢ less, or $7.48, and therefore your change should be 2¢ more, or $2.52. This method uses a general idea about the operation of addition, the claim that these two expressions are equivalent:

$$\$7.50 + \$2.50 = \$7.48 + \$2.52$$

The person making this calculation probably doesn't explicitly think about why these two expressions are equivalent—the reasoning involved may be virtually automatic. We could write down the underlying generalization explicitly as follows:

> If you subtract an amount from one addend and add the same amount to another addend, the sum remains the same.

$$\$7.50 + \$2.50 = (\$7.50 - \$.02) + (\$2.50 + \$.02) = \$7.48 + \$2.52$$

Students learn procedures that are based on just such generalizations, but they may learn them only as steps that work, without understanding why the steps make sense. In the elementary grades, some students notice and use these kinds of ideas in their computation all the time, but too often, generalizations are not made explicit for the class as a whole. By focusing on making and justifying generalizations in the context of arithmetic, students are supported in building a more complex grasp of the operations. This knowledge will build computational fluency and, in later grades, facilitate the transition from arithmetic to algebra.

THE FIRST STEP FOR THE TEACHER: NOTICING

Generalizing about an arithmetic operation may be a new and unfamiliar focus for you and your students. But generalizing in the context of arithmetic is not *extra* content. Rather, students are already using general ideas about the operations as they solve addition, subtraction, multiplication, and division problems. These generalizations may come up implicitly or explicitly as students observe patterns or discover regularity. You may notice students using a rule without explicitly stating it, or you may hear students express particular generalizations and use them. For example, a student working on addition problems might say, "I know that 6 plus 4 equals 10, so 4 plus 6 equals 10—you can turn the numbers around and it makes the same thing."

Paying attention to opportunities for generalizing that emerge from students' work is the first step in making these important ideas a regular part of instruction. What generalizations are expressed during students' computation? What underlying generalizations are students using without thinking about them explicitly? Looking at your students' work through this lens can help you identify generalizations about operations that might be fruitful for your class to investigate. As you read the following example, consider how one grade 5 teacher sets up an activity in which students are likely to notice patterns, notes what students notice, then builds on one idea that comes up.

Grade 5

Near the beginning of the year, Marlena Diaz engages her fifth graders in a Number of the Day activity. She asks students to write a list of addition expressions equivalent to 32 in their math journals. She deliberately picks a number that her students can work with easily because her focus is not on the computation itself but on generalizing about addition. As she walks around the class observing students' writing, she notices that Sean has the following written in his journal:

$$30 + 2$$

$$29 + 3$$

$$28 + 4$$

She posts his sequence on the board, and asks students to consider it.

⋯⋯⋯⋯⋯⋯⋯⋯⋯⋯⋯⋯⋯⋯⋯⋯⋯⋯⋯⋯⋯

Christy: We can keep going. Add "27 plus 5."

Lateia [coming up and pointing]: See these keep going down and these keep going up.

Ms. Diaz: Why do you think that is happening? Talk in your table groups for a while.

After a few minutes of student discussion:

Ms. Diaz: So what do you think is happening?

Kathryn: Well, you take some from one number and give it to another.

Amelia: All that is happening is that you are moving some amounts around. And it stays the same.

Christy: You aren't adding any or taking any away.

Eddie: Right. It is like if you had two groups of dots. We just are changing the size of the groups.

Sean: And since all numbers are made up of ones, we can just move all those ones around.

Jonah: And we are going to get to a point where it won't work anymore. When we get to 16 plus 16.

Sean: Right, then it will start all over again. It will repeat but basically it is the same numbers switched around.

⋯⋯⋯⋯⋯⋯⋯⋯⋯⋯⋯⋯⋯⋯⋯⋯⋯⋯⋯⋯⋯

In the grade 5 class, as students look at Sean's list, they begin to describe what is consistent in all the expressions:

"You take from one number and give it to another."

"You are moving some amounts around. And it stays the same."

"You aren't adding any or taking any away."

The students at first notice the *pattern* in their series of expressions: 30 + 2, 29 + 3, 28 + 4, and so on. Lateia observes, "These keep going down and these keep going up," referring to the two columns of numbers. The conversation could have remained at the level of making observations about what the pattern *looks like*. But the teacher asks her students, "Why do you think that is happening?" to focus them on reasoning about the relationship among these expressions.

The discussion is just beginning for these students. They have much engaging work to do as they investigate further. Eddie's idea about visualizing two groups of dots will provide a mechanism for the class to explain *why* this generalization works. Representations such as drawings, models, number lines, groups of objects, rectangular arrays, and so forth are the tools that are available to young students for reasoning about general claims they are making about an operation. As students continue their discussions, the teacher will work with them to articulate a clear statement of their idea, such as the one articulated earlier for the problem $4.99 + $2.49. (Look back at that problem and think about its relationship to these fifth graders' ideas.) They will represent their idea in a variety of ways and move toward proving that their idea holds true for *any* addition problem. They will develop a strong foundation for applying general rules with understanding in their computation work and, later, in the realm of algebra.

The first step, then, is to notice general ideas that occur in the course of your regular computation instruction. Here are two brief examples of students solving arithmetic problems at the beginning of the year. As these teachers get to know their students and how they think about numbers and operations, the teachers also notice generalizations that are either implicit or explicit in students' work. As you read the examples, keep these questions in mind:

1. What relationships between two arithmetic expressions are students noticing?

2. If you were the teacher in one of these classrooms, what questions might you ask to help students pursue these beginning ideas further?

Grade 1

Emma Perkins is working on an activity called "How Many of Each?" with her class.[1] The problem she poses is, "You have 10 vegetables on your plate. Some are

---

1 Russell, Susan Jo, Economopoulos, Karen, Wittenberg, Lucy, et al. (2008). *Investigations in Number, Data, and Space*. Second edition. Glenview, IL: Pearson Scott Foresman.

peas and some are carrots. How many peas and how many carrots could you have?"
Ms. Perkins writes:

> *Each child counted out beans, which were green on one side and orange on the*
> *other. All of the students settled on 5 + 5 = 10 as the answer. I got blank faces when*
> *I asked if there was another way to solve the problem. It seemed as if these children*
> *were used to getting one answer and moving on to the next part of the lesson.*
> *But I wasn't ready, and I could wait a long time. After repeating my question for*
> *a different solution, Harriet played with her beans and said "9 plus 1 equals 10,"*
> *which she wrote on her paper. Mikel then decided that 7 + 3 = 10 would be another*
> *answer. Connor complained, "I was going to write that." I suggested that they both*
> *could put it down and waited to see what might happen. As it turned out, Mikel*
> *wrote 7 + 3 = 10 and Connor wrote 3 + 7 = 10, creating a great opportunity for*
> *comparing these two expressions.*

Grade 4

At the beginning of the year, Marie Taft establishes a routine called "What Do You
Know About ___?" She puts an expression on the board and asks students to tell her
what they know about the number it equals without doing any computation. Like
Marlena Diaz, Ms. Taft uses numbers that are easily accessible to her students so that
they can focus on relationships between expressions. The previous day, students had
discussed the expression 4×10. In order to build on that discussion, Ms. Taft writes *4*
× 20 on the board. Here is part of the conversation she documented:

⋯⋯⋯⋯⋯⋯⋯⋯⋯⋯⋯⋯⋯⋯⋯⋯⋯⋯⋯⋯

Ms. Taft: What do you know about 4 times 20?

Jasmine: I know it is even just like 4 times 10 because both of the numbers are
even, just like 4 times 10.

Faith: I know that it is going to be more than 4 times 10 because 20 is double 10.

Ms. Taft: Can you tell me more about that?

> *Most hands shot up at this point, so I had partners talk to each other about it*
> *again. When the discussion lightened, I asked someone to explain what Faith*
> *meant.*

Billy: It is just double 4 times 10 because 20 is double 10. It is like if you give 4 kids
10 pencils, and then give them 10 more, you have given them 20, and 20 is double
10.

⋯⋯⋯⋯⋯⋯⋯⋯⋯⋯⋯⋯⋯⋯⋯⋯⋯⋯⋯⋯

In these two examples, teachers are learning what their students know at the
beginning of the year. As part of this work, the teachers set up situations in which

they can pay attention to what students notice about the behavior of the operations. What might these teachers be noticing?

In the grade 1 "How Many of Each?" activity, students generate addition expressions equivalent to 10. Given more such opportunities, will students notice that $3 + 7$ and $7 + 3$ are both equivalent to 10? Will they notice other pairs of expressions, such as $1 + 9$ and $9 + 1$? Will they conjecture that changing the order of the addends does not change the sum, not just for 10 but for any number (the commutative property of addition)?

In the grade 4 episode, students notice something about the relationship between 4×10 and 4×20. One student knows that the product of 4×20 will be greater than the product of 4×10 "because 20 is double 10." Another conjectures about how much more 4×20 is than 4×10. Billy makes an important contribution, offering an image to support his conjecture, "It is like if you give 4 kids 10 pencils, and then give them 10 more, you have given them 20, and 20 is double 10."

Will students extend their thinking beyond the particular numbers to notice that doubling one factor in any multiplication expression doubles the product? With additional focus on this idea, will students be able to articulate and demonstrate why this occurs? Will they become interested in investigating what happens to the product if both factors are doubled?

Ms. Perkins and Ms. Taft are noticing ideas their students might pursue in the context of the year's work on computation and operations. Ms. Perkins notices an idea implicit in students' work that the students themselves may not yet have recognized. Ms. Taft notices some students articulating an idea that can lead to a conjecture about multiplication. Ms. Diaz leads a discussion in which students start to articulate a general idea about the operation of addition. The general ideas you notice in your students' work become the starting points for engagement in generalizing about the operations. ■

GENERALIZING IN ARITHMETIC: GETTING STARTED, PART I—NOTICING

1. The first section of Chapter 1 makes the case that elementary math study should include opportunities for students to investigate general ideas about the operations they use in their computation work. As you reflect on this passage (pages 1–3), consider the following questions.

    • What examples from your own classroom come to mind?

    • Do these paragraphs suggest shifts you might want to try in your own practice?

    • What questions does this passage raise?

2. The beginning of the second section of Chapter 1 states that having students generalize in the context of arithmetic should not be seen as extra or additional content but as a regular focus of the class, enhancing the work already included in the curriculum.

    • What are your thoughts about that statement?

    • What are the implications of that statement?

    • How might that work in your classroom?

3. Consider the student discussion from Marlena Diaz's class as an opportunity to analyze student thinking and teacher moves.

    • What does Lateia offer the class?

    • What are the contributions of Kathyrn, Amelia, Christy, and Eddie?

    • Explain what Jonah and Sean notice.

    • Examine the actions and questions of Ms. Diaz. Consider what her purpose might be for each of these.

4. Consider the examples from Emma Perkins' grade 1 and Marie Taft's grade 4.

    • In each example, what are the arithmetic expressions to be compared? What generalizations might be examined on the basis of these comparisons?

    • If you were the teacher in one of these classrooms, what questions might you ask to help students pursue these beginning ideas further?

2

Generalizing in Arithmetic

*Getting Started, Part II—Helping Students
Share What They Notice*

Once you start to notice the generalizations that students use, you may be surprised at how many opportunities for generalizing emerge from your students' work. This chapter discusses two more steps to incorporate generalizing into your mathematics instruction: *helping students learn to share what they notice* about the general ideas implicit in their study of computation and operations, and *planning regular instructional opportunities* to engage students explicitly in this work.

THE SECOND STEP: HELPING STUDENTS LEARN TO SHARE WHAT THEY NOTICE

The development of regular opportunities for students to share with their classmates what they notice about the operations is critical to incorporating generalizing into classroom work. Through such sharing, students help each other make sense of an idea, work together to articulate precisely what they mean, demonstrate with different representations, and eventually prove their claims. To establish a classroom in which students engage in these activities, teachers must help students learn to participate in such mathematical discussions and to understand that the regularities they are noticing are, in fact, an important aspect of mathematics.

While the teachers described in Chapter 1 were working on noticing generalizations, they were also establishing expectations for doing mathematics in their classrooms. They used these lessons early in the year to model the kinds of questions they expect students to consider, the ways in which students participate in mathematics, how students interact with each other during class discussions, and how to keep the focus on mathematical ideas, representations, and relationships.

During the first part of the school year, it is critical to establish a classroom community in which students' mathematical thinking is valued, students are willing to publicly try out incomplete ideas, and students listen to and build on each other's thinking. To make mathematics discussions that focus on identifying, describing, and justifying consistencies across problems the norm, teachers:

- make it clear to students that they are interested in what the students notice about numbers, arithmetic expressions, and operations, and

- discuss with students how the class mathematics discussions are going, how to improve them, and what prevents students from participating fully.

Letting Students Know You're Interested

Students joining your classroom have varied conceptions of what it means to do mathematics. It is important to establish immediately that mathematics is about ideas, that all the students in the class are capable of having ideas in mathematics, and that all are expected to contribute to the development of the class' ideas. Students must learn that ideas need not be fully formed to be expressed; tentative ideas provide important beginnings.

Start the year with discussion openers that invite a range of responses to reassure students that they have something to contribute. Openers often begin with a question of the form, "What do you know about _____?" focusing on a number, operation, or expression accessible to the students. Teachers use these discussions to establish an atmosphere of collegiality and investigation, assess what students know, listen to the mathematical ideas students have, consider what problem areas are evident in what students say, and choose content that may be worth pursuing. Here are two examples.

Teacher Corie Olana wants to start the first day of her fourth-grade class with work on multiplication. Before doing so, she poses a straightforward question to assess what her students know:

Ms. Olana: We are going to write expressions that equal today's number: 16. But before we do that, I want people to share some facts you know about 16.

Samuel: 16 is an even number.

Darnell: 16 is a multiple of 3.

Samir: When you double 16, you get a high number.

Ms. Olana: What "high number" will you get when you double 16?

Blanca: You get 32.

Claudia: 16 is a 2-digit number.

Aman: You can double 8 to get 16.

Darnell: I know there is a 10 in 16.

Samuel: There are 16 ones, the 10 is 10 ones plus the 6 ones.

Ms. Olana: We are going to continue adding to the list as we learn more things about 16. But before we continue, let's clarify some information we listed. Darnell said that 16 is a multiple of 3. Do we all agree to that?

The open-ended and accessible question—"What do you know about 16?"—provides an inviting entry for the students. The teacher notices who is contributing, what ideas students hold solidly, and where there are confusions. For example, Ms. Olana noted the following:

- Claudia is a new student to the school. Ms. Olana was impressed at her boldness, raising her hand and volunteering answers.

- Samir asserted that 16 doubled is "a high number": what is his sense of the magnitude of 16 or 32 as compared to other numbers?

- No other students challenged Darnell's statement that 16 is a multiple of 3. Perhaps they also think 3 is a factor of 16, or perhaps they do not yet know how to disagree, or that it is possible to disagree in math class.

Open-ended discussions structured around accessible questions provide student-generated material from which the teacher can formulate further questions to pursue. Initially, questions will focus on particular numbers and particular problems; eventually, the teacher's questions will bring students' attention to generalizations.

The second example comes from a third-grade class. Early in the year the teacher, Alice Kaye, decides to find out what her students know and can articulate about the operations. She begins one of the class' first mathematics conversations by asking students directly what they know about addition and subtraction, using the following chart.

$6 + 3 = 9$ What does ADDITION mean?	$7 - 2 = 5$ What does SUBTRACTION mean?

....

Ms. Kaye: I want to hear from you. When you hear 6 plus 3 equals 9, what comes to mind? What picture do you get? What actions do you connect with it?

Clarissa: Addition is when you're going to add things on.

Ms. Kaye: And what's another word for *add*? Can you substitute another word for what you mean by *add*? Clarissa, call on someone who thinks she or he can pick up on the thread you started.

Helen: A different word for *add* could be . . . like plussing on.

Allie: It's kind of like putting together.

> *This is the first idea I heard that seemed to indicate an action rather than refer to the "plus" symbol. At this point I started to record on the chart all of the ideas that had been offered thus far.*

Ms. Kaye: Does anyone else have another idea for what *addition* means? Sierra, did you have another idea for what *addition* means?

Sierra [*after a long pause*]**:** It's like you have two numbers . . . [*another long pause*] . . . I think I need a little more time.

> *At this point, I also made a big deal of her being courageous and trusting enough to ask for what she needed. I talked about how good it felt to know that already this class was becoming the kind of place where people could do what they needed for themselves as learners and that we'd all be okay with it.*

Helen: It's like putting one number on top of the other, like snap cubes.

Ms. Kaye: Were you thinking of a model or something you could show with the snap cubes?

....

The conversations in both examples gave many students a chance to participate. The use of open-ended and accessible questions helped to set both a tone for mathematical discussions that invites students to contribute and an expectation that they communicate what they know and notice about numbers and operations.

At the same time, the discussions provided teachers with information about the students' ideas. On the basis of this information, teachers will be able to formulate new questions that move them into the territory of generalizations.

Note that the questions in these examples would be appropriate for a variety of grade levels, though the range of responses would be different.

Discussing Your Discussions

It's important to discuss the effectiveness of your mathematics discussions throughout the year, but especially during the first two months of school. Consider the following fifth-grade class on the seventh day of school. From the first day of the year, the teacher, Marlena Diaz, has been listening to students' observations. She encourages the class to, as she puts it, "talk about their talking" regularly.

⋯⋯⋯⋯⋯⋯⋯⋯⋯⋯⋯⋯⋯⋯⋯⋯⋯⋯⋯⋯⋯

Ms. Diaz: Remember how I told you the first day of school that we would be having lots of conversations in math class this year, and how I wanted you all to work on listening and responding to each others' ideas? I would like you to take a few seconds to think about how you think our discussions are going.

Kathryn: One of the things I like is that there are lots of kids talking, and that keeps me interested so I don't feel like I am going to fall asleep like I have in other classes.

Will: Well, I think we are doing pretty good when we are getting our voices loud so others can hear us. But some people are only looking at you [*indicating the teacher*] when they are talking.

Ms. Diaz: Yes, that is an important point. Why should we try to improve on that?

Keila: Because you can see if people are listening to you and if they can hear you and know your ideas.

Ms. Diaz: Sure, when you are sharing your ideas you can pay attention to how everyone is listening to you and you can invite someone to add to your thinking or ask them if they understand.

At this point there was a long silence and no one was sharing.

Ms. Diaz: So we are having a discussion about how our talking in math is going, but no one is talking! [*We all laugh here!*] **Is this question hard? Have you ever spent time thinking about how you participate in discussions? Like what do you do when something is hard for you to think about? Or when you don't get what someone is saying?**

Kathryn: Well, no one has ever asked me to think about this before. Usually, it is like we just have to have silence.

Ms. Diaz: When I was in school, we didn't spend time talking. Only the teacher did the thinking. But I want us to be a team so that we all can contribute.

Will: I like how we show our thinking, you know like we come up to the overhead and show our thinking. I like how lots of people have different ideas.

Brent: It is like there are lots of teachers.

Ms. Diaz: What are some things you do when you don't understand someone?

Cole: I might ask them to say it again.

Lateia: You could ask them to say it with different words.

Eddie: I should ask questions.

Ms. Diaz: So that is one thing that I haven't seen us doing a lot yet is asking each other questions. And you know it is OK to ask questions and to say you disagree. It is not because you don't like the person's thinking, but because you are interested in how their idea goes with yours.

Juan: I still am a little scared that someone might laugh at me.

Ms. Diaz: What do the rest of you think about Juan's comment?

Here Ms. Diaz welcomes whatever students say about how they think the discussions are going. She follows up on points she thinks are important for everyone to think about more deeply ("Why should we try to improve on that?"). She poses the specific question, "What are some things you do when you don't understand someone?" She knows this is a common situation for students, but that they might be reluctant to bring it up themselves.

Once it has become clear to students that they are expected both to participate and to reflect periodically on their participation, students and teacher can refer to classroom norms and expectations without stopping the mathematics work. In fact, remarking on students' participation at the moment that something occurs helps them better understand what behaviors are valued and productive and why. Think back to Ms. Kaye's third-grade class (pp. 11–12). Ms. Kaye remarked immediately on Sierra's willingness to say she needed more time to think out her ideas. Following is another example.

As the year begins, Lydia Rogers leads her fourth graders in a discussion about factors and multiples. Nick raises his hand and appears excited, but when he begins to speak, he can't articulate what he wants to say. Ms. Rogers describes what happened:

It's cumbersome to keep the terms [e.g., factors, multiples] straight for students at this age and Nick becomes tongue-tied. Because I'm unsure about what he is trying to say, I ask if he can explain it again. He starts, but by now he has lost the connection he was about to make. He smiles broadly.

Nick: I don't know what I'm talking about!

We all start to laugh together, not at Nick, but at the recognition of something that happens to all of us.

Ms. Rogers: I think we just learned the most valuable lesson we'll have today. Does anyone know what it might be?

Bella: That it's OK not to know what you are talking about?

We all laugh again. I watch Bella carefully to be sure she knows we are not laughing at her. She seems comfortable.

Sean: That it's OK to make mistakes.

Students: It was funny . . . That happens to me all the time. . . .

Ms. Rogers: I think Nick was very brave to let us see inside his brain *[lots of giggles]* **as it's still trying to figure something out. It's hard to have people notice when you don't understand something. Nick, we are still very interested in what you think you were thinking** *[more giggles]*, **so would you like to work with Sean to see if together you can put your ideas back together?**

Ms. Rogers takes this opportunity to point out that becoming confused, not being able to articulate an idea, and losing track of one's thoughts are all part of the work they will be doing together throughout the year. What is important is that Nick is having ideas and trying to articulate them. The teacher and class will benefit from Nick working his ideas out and expressing them. By sending him off with Sean, Ms. Rogers makes it clear that collaboration and interaction are supports that can help individuals work through their ideas.

Many classrooms develop lists of general guidelines for discussions. These usually include rules such as "Raise your hand," "Don't interrupt," or "Be respectful of others' opinions." Such general guidelines can be a good beginning, but students need to delve into specific examples about discussion in mathematics and have multiple opportunities to consider what makes a discussion or activity work for themselves and others as the mathematics community develops. Because many students may not have experienced discussion in mathematics that focuses on the investigation of ideas rather than the sharing of answers or strategies, this work requires time and persistence. Over the first months of school, the teachers in the previous examples move from focusing on general rules of respectful conversation to a consideration of more specific behaviors that support the generation, expansion, and critique of mathematical ideas.

We next focus on *planning regular instructional opportunities* to engage students in considering general ideas about an operation, articulating general rules, and investigating when they apply and why they occur.

THE THIRD STEP: PLANNING OPPORTUNITIES FOR GENERALIZING

While first learning how to integrate generalizing into instruction, many teachers use a classroom routine that provides a regular structure for this kind of investigation. They allocate a regular time several days each week—ten to fifteen minutes or longer—to noticing generalizations. Creating this regular routine helps students develop the habit of noticing, articulating, and investigating generalizations.

Following are three examples of such routines. Each provides an opportunity to engage students in considering one or more expressions or equations specifically chosen because they are examples of an underlying generalization. It is often helpful to choose one routine and use it repeatedly for a while. As students become used to the routine and the kinds of questions you ask them to consider, they become more willing to offer ideas, observations, and conjectures. Over time, the class develops a repertoire of ideas the students have noticed and conjectures they have made.

What Do You Know About _____?

Asking what students know about an expression can be a good way to start the year because it invites a range of student observations and provides a window into the understandings and experiences students bring to the classroom. It is also useful throughout the year because you can choose expressions that connect to whatever ideas students are currently studying. For this routine, the teacher carefully chooses an expression or sequence of related expressions to bring out particular mathematical ideas. For example, as you saw in Chapter 1, Marie Taft (pp. 6–7) asked her students, "What do you know about 4 times 10?" then followed up the next day by asking, "What do you know about 4 times 20?" She knew that comparing the two expressions would lead students to move toward this generalization: When one factor of a multiplication expression is doubled, the product doubles. In subsequent sessions, she might ask, "What do you know about 8 times 10?" or "What do you know about 4 times 40?" Gradually, students notice a pattern in what is happening as a factor is doubled. Then they can begin the work of more clearly articulating a conjecture and investigating whether and why it is always true. You can choose operations and expressions appropriate to your own grade level and content.

Number of the Day

In this routine, students are asked to generate expressions equivalent to a particular number. Some teachers use the day's date (that is, on October 12, the Number of the Day is 12), others use the school day's number (that is, on the twentieth day of school, the number is 20), and some teachers choose numbers specific to the content they want to emphasize. Teachers have used this basic routine for decades, and it appears in a number of elementary mathematics curricula. It provides a good context for generalizing.

Teachers may ask students to write their own individual list of expressions first. Then the teacher strategically chooses expressions to share that are productive for the whole class to think about. Ms. Diaz does this when she chooses Sean's sequence of expressions for the whole class to consider—30 + 2, 29 + 3, 28 + 4 (Chapter 1, pp. 4–5). At other times, teachers ask students to generate expressions during whole-class discussion. The teacher can then draw students' attention to particular expressions.

At first, this routine can be quite open-ended—students are asked to generate whatever expressions they can think of. Later, to focus on particular regularities across expressions, the teacher may add constraints. For example, the teacher might require students to use more than two addends, to use a particular operation or combination of operations, or include a three-digit number or a fraction. Like the first routine, these choices are made because the teacher has in mind a generalization that will be fruitful for students to work on. Or the teacher may want students to reconsider whether a generalization they have already considered still holds with larger numbers or fractions.

For example, the Number of the Day is 12 in Isabel Hazelton's second-grade class, and she has asked her students to use only the operation of subtraction. The class quickly comes up with the following expressions:

$$12 - 0$$

$$13 - 1$$

$$14 - 2$$

$$15 - 3$$

Soon her students want to discuss what they are seeing.

....

Connor: It keeps going on by 1. Like 12 minus 0 and 13 minus 1; it just keeps going on by 1.

Becky: That's one thing that I'm wondering about. Why does it happen?

....

These second graders are on their way to exploring the generalization: If both numbers of a subtraction expression increase by 1, the difference remains the same.

Is the Number Sentence True?

In this routine, students consider equality and inequality. Students are shown two expressions connected by an equal sign, and asked: Is the number sentence true?

Teachers generally start with quite small numbers so that students can learn the format of the routine, for example, $8 + 4 = 9 + 3$. There are two important points that students need to understand to engage with this routine. First, they need to understand that an expression, not just a single number, can appear on the right of the equal sign. If students have seen only single numbers on the right (e.g., $8 + 4 = 12$), they may think of the equal sign as a signal that means "now write down the answer" rather than an indication of equality (see Chapter 7 for more about students' understanding of the equal sign). Second, as they get used to the routine, they learn that the teacher is asking them to reason about why the two expressions are, or are not, equal without computing each expression. That is, it is easy to assert that $8 + 4 = 9 + 3$ is true because both expressions are equivalent to 12. However, simply computing the result of each expression does not move students toward considering an underlying generalization of which this equation is an example: In an addition expression, if one addend is increased by 1 and another addend is decreased by 1, the sum remains the same.

Lorraine Vasquez has been using this routine with her fourth graders. At first, she asked them to consider small numbers they could easily visualize. In this session, she has decided to present an equation with three-digit numbers. She writes on the board:

$$425 + 315 = 430 + 310$$

···

Ms. Vasquez: Is this true or not? I want you to think about it without solving the problem.

Fleurette: How can we do that without solving it?

Ms. Vasquez: Look carefully at these numbers. What do you notice about them?

Fleurette: Yes, it is true because 25 plus 15 is 40, and 30 plus 10 is 40, and since the 4 hundred and the 3 hundred stay the same in both sides, it is the same.

Malik: It is true. 400 plus 300 equals 700, 20 plus 10 equals 30, 5 plus 5 equals 10. 740. And the other one is also 740.

Ms. Vasquez: Oh! So you solved the problem.

Rose: It is true because the 5 from 315 goes into 425.

Ms. Vasquez: So what happens with the quantities? How do they change?

Rose: Take the 5 from 315, give it to 425, that turns into 430 and the other one turns into 310.

Elizabeth: We are not taking away anything; we are shifting numbers.

Ms. Vasquez: What if Ms. Raymond or Ms. Perez comes in the room and says she doesn't understand, or she doesn't even trust what you are saying. How could you convince her that this equality is true? How can you prove it is true? You can use drawings, cubes, or a story to convince her.

···

Students now work in pairs to come up with a story context or model. One student creates a story like this: "There are 315 kids in the school. There are 425 in another school. 5 of the kids went to the other school, so now there's 310 and 430. We still have the same amount, but we changed the numbers." Elizabeth and Rose use base ten blocks to build 315 and 425. Then they shift 5 unit blocks from the 315 to the 425. They explain that they have the same amount as before, but just shifted the 5 from one group to the other without adding any more blocks or taking any away.

Underlying these students' work is a broader generalization related to the one mentioned above about adding and subtracting 1: In an addition expression, if one addend is increased by some amount and another addend is decreased by the same amount, the sum remains the same. Ms. Vasquez plans to do further work with her students, presenting other examples like this one within the routine, to help them articulate and investigate this generalization.

This excerpt illustrates how unfamiliar it is for these students to think about relationships of equality without carrying out the computation for each expression. At any grade level, it takes time for students to build other strategies for comparing expressions. Through regular use of the routine, students begin to share ways to compare two expressions without computing the result for each, as Rose and Elizabeth do in this excerpt. Gradually, students learn to develop and justify mathematical arguments based on images and models. Asking questions that require reasoning about problems without computing requires students to think more deeply about the operations.

Some teachers use variations of the "Is the Number Sentence True?" routine:

Which expression is greater?

$$20 - 6 \qquad 21 - 5$$

How do you know they're equal?

$$5 \times 100 \qquad 50 \times 10$$

The purpose of the questions is to emphasize the relationship between the two expressions. Without computing, how would you answer the questions?

GUIDELINES FOR FOCUSING ON GENERALIZATION IN THE CLASSROOM

The following four strategies can help focus students' attention on generalizing about the operations.

1. Choose accessible numbers when asking students to investigate general ideas about the operations.

The purpose of these routines is not simply to carry out the operations but to notice and explore generalizations by analyzing mathematical relationships and consistencies across problems. For this reason, teachers keep the numbers quite manageable so that the focus can shift to reasoning about *why* the two expressions are equivalent or not. For example, Ms. Diaz (pp. 4–5) chose arithmetic expressions (30 + 2, 29 + 3, 28 + 4) that her fifth graders could visualize easily because she wanted them to focus on the relationships between expressions, what is true *generally* of these expressions, and *what accounts* for the consistencies they are noticing. By working at first with these manageable numbers, students are less likely to become overwhelmed and can concentrate on generalizing across problems. Later, when they have considered a number of examples and have articulated their ideas, they can apply the generalization to larger or less familiar numbers.

2. Ask students to think about an expression or a set of related expressions without carrying out the computation.

When asked to compare two expressions to determine which is greater or whether they are equal, the natural impulse of most students is to carry out the computation to compare them. Students are unsure how they can make such a comparison without relying on the computed result of each expression: 30 + 2 is equivalent to 29 + 3 because both have a sum of 32. Not only do students find comfort in carrying out familiar computation procedures, but they may actually not understand at first what they are being asked to do. As Fleurette, Ms. Vasquez's student, says, "How can we do that without solving it?" Regardless of grade level, students may never have been asked to think about the equality or inequality of two expressions by reasoning about their relationship rather than computing the results.

Teachers have found that, as the year goes on and these discussions occur routinely, students begin to offer ways to compare two expressions without computing, as Rose and Elizabeth do in Ms. Vasquez's class. Gradually, students learn to develop mathematical arguments, based on images and models, to justify both particular examples and general statements across many examples.

3. Ask students to show their ideas using cubes, number lines, arrays, story contexts, or other representations.

To think about general claims about operations and investigate *why* these claims are true, students need some way to represent each operation and examine its action. For example, as Ms. Diaz's class worked on related addition expressions (pp. 4–5), Eddie referred to a mental image: "It is like if you had two groups of dots. We just are changing the size of the groups." Eddie is offering the class a familiar way to picture addition as the joining of two groups; if dots are moved from one group to another, the size of the groups changes but the total number of dots remains the same. Likewise, in Ms. Taft's class (p. 6), Billy used a story context to explain his idea about the relationship between 4×10 and 4×20: "It is like if you give 4 kids 10 pencils, and then give them 10 more, you have given them 20 and 20 is double 10." Ms. Vasquez's students used a story context and base ten blocks to model how the sum of two quantities does not change.

These representations offer students ways to visualize the action of the operations, see relationships between expressions, explain their ideas, and later, justify their general claims. It is often difficult for students to explain their ideas well orally, even when they have a clear idea about what they are trying to say, and it can be equally difficult for others to follow their words. The use of models, representations, and story contexts makes ideas visible and public, helps students clarify and articulate their own ideas, and gives access to more students to consider and build on those ideas. Facility with representations for each operation is key to pursuing work on generalization, as you will see in many of the classroom examples to follow. In particular, Chapters 5 and 8 illustrate the use of representations and story contexts to prove general claims.

4. Keep a list of ideas in progress.

To keep track of ideas that emerge from students' thinking, teachers keep a list of conjectures emerging from their discussions. A *conjecture* is a statement that has been proposed as true and appears to be correct but has not yet been proven or disproven. The list might be called "Rules We Think Are True."

By the twentieth day of school, Ms. Diaz's fifth graders have compiled conjectures including:

- All numbers can be broken up into different-sized pieces and those pieces can be added in many different ways.

- The pieces can be fractions, and now we can include many other ways to combine.

- If you are adding two numbers and you add an amount to one number and you take that same amount from the other number, then your total does not change.

- When you multiply two numbers you get a bigger number, but we aren't sure about numbers less than 1.

- All numbers in a multiplication problem can be written with prime numbers.

Such public lists of ideas in progress let students know that considering conjectures is an important part of math class. As the year goes on, the class revisits ideas as they arise in new contexts or with new classes of numbers such as fractions or negative numbers. When selecting conjectures to revisit, the teacher chooses ideas from the list that support particular topics in the curriculum or are fundamental to students' understanding of an operation. After some conjectures have been satisfactorily proven to be true, these can be moved to another list of mathematical ideas the class takes to be true and can rely on. You will read more about how students prove that a generalization is true in Chapters 5 and 8.

IN CONCLUSION . . .

So far we have provided an orientation to generalizing in the context of arithmetic instruction and some processes for becoming aware and making students aware of consistencies and regularities in the behavior of mathematical operations. In the next chapter, we focus on how teachers establish a mathematics community in which articulating, representing, and justifying general claims are a regular part of mathematics instruction for all learners in the class, including those having difficulty and those excelling in grade-level computation. ■

FOCUS QUESTIONS

GENERALIZING IN ARITHMETIC: GETTING STARTED, PART II—HELPING STUDENTS SHARE WHAT THEY NOTICE

1. In the first section of Chapter 2, we visit four teachers' classrooms (Ms. Olana, Ms. Kaye, Ms. Diaz, and Ms. Rogers). Locate a particular passage for each teacher in which you notice the teacher working to help her students learn how to have math discussions. Take notes on the specific actions or words of the teacher including the impact on students, if any. What are the implications of these teacher moves for your own classroom?

2. The next section of Chapter 2 details some examples of routines that teachers can use to provide opportunities for their students to investigate generalizations.

   • If you have used such routines previously, what is the same and what is different about the examples in the chapter in comparison to your past experiences?

   • What routine might you try and what is it you would like to learn by implementing it?

3. In this chapter we see teachers asking their students to answer mathematical questions without carrying out the indicated computation, and presenting them with numbers that are quite accessible. Yet, the teacher's goal is to support the development of their students as mathematical thinkers. Find examples that illustrate how reasoning without calculating highlights important mathematical ideas for the students.

3

Generalizing in Arithmetic
with a Range of Learners

The classroom examples in this chapter follow students with a range of strengths and needs in mathematics. These learners cannot and should not be classified simply as "high," "low," and "average." They respond differently depending on the context, the problem, the questions being asked, and the nature of interactions with the teacher and with their classmates. This chapter is intended to help you become more aware of how students with different strengths and needs can participate in and benefit from a focus on the behaviors and properties of the operations.

Consider these questions as you read the examples: How do teachers engage all students in generalizing about the operations, including those who are struggling with grade-level computation and those who find that content unchallenging? What is the value of this work for students with different strengths and needs in mathematics? How do students with differing sets of strengths contribute to the thinking of the class as a whole?

EPISODE A: "I WAS THINKING ABOUT ADDITION, BUT IT WAS SUPPOSED TO BE ABOUT SUBTRACTION."

In Isabel Hazelton's second-grade class, students have been generating addition expressions in a "Number of the Day" activity. Some students begin generating subtraction expressions on their own. However, when Ms. Hazelton changes the focus of the "Number of the Day" task to generating subtraction expressions equivalent to 4, some students are stumped. They know how to use subtraction to solve story problems that involve starting with some quantity and then removing part of that quantity, but starting with the *difference* and working backward does not make sense to them.

Here is part of the teacher's account of the discussion. As you read, focus particularly on the contributions of Sean, Ben, Jocelyn, and Claude. What do you notice about each student's thinking? What ideas does each student add to the discussion? Jot down your thoughts about how each student contributes to the discussion.

....

Ms. Hazelton: So let's just talk about what subtraction means to people. Are there thoughts?

Sean: I know how you can use subtraction if it's hard for you. If you have to get to 4 and you have 8, you just count backwards from 8 to 4 and just take away how many numbers you counted backwards. So you can count onto 4 how many numbers and then how many you have to take away you count backwards . . . like to see how far. . . .

> *Sean got stuck here. My sense was that he was trying to say that you count on to 4 until you reach another number. Then count back that same amount to return to 4.*

Ms. Hazelton: You kind of lost track of your idea? *[Sean nods.]* **Hmm. Can anyone say what they think Sean is talking about or does anyone have a question for Sean?**

Ben: What does he mean about it? I'm confused.

> *I noticed bodies begin to shift, a sure sign that it was getting hard for some to listen. But I feel this discussion about subtraction is important, and I try to reengage the students in the discussion.*

Ms. Hazelton: These ideas are so hard that some people are even having a hard time sitting here thinking about it. I'm hoping that we can think about it a little bit longer to help each other out.

Ben: I'm thinking of something else. I just know that subtraction is backwards addition and addition is backwards subtraction . . . *[as his voice trails off, Ben adds]* and division is backwards multiplication.

Ms. Hazelton: So you don't know why that is and what causes that to happen but that's how you think about them? *[Ben nods.]* **Could somebody repeat what Ben just said?**

Jocelyn: Subtraction is like the opposite from addition. So it's like backwards addition and backwards subtraction.

Ms. Hazelton: What do you mean by *backwards subtraction*?

Jocelyn: It's like backwards subtraction, because it's like subtraction to 1 and addition to 10.

> As Jocelyn speaks, she uses her hand to draw imaginary lines in the air. She motions from right to left with her right hand to show subtraction. Then she motions from left to right with her left hand to show addition. I notice that some students, including Claude, missed Jocelyn's demonstration.

Ms. Hazelton: Did everyone see what Jocelyn was doing with her hands just now? Let's look again.

Jocelyn: I said subtraction's backwards from, the opposite from addition, because addition goes to 10 higher [*points with her left hand from left to right*] and subtraction is going to 1 lower [*pointing with her right hand from right to left*].

Ms. Hazelton: When Jocelyn was pointing her hands, it reminded me a little bit of a number line. Jocelyn, what were you thinking of?

Jocelyn: I just had a picture like of a piece of paper and I only saw 1 to 10. Sort of like a number line.

Ms. Hazelton [*drawing a number line from 1 to 10 on the board*]: **So even though a number line could go past 10, you were only thinking from 1 to 10. Then what were you thinking?**

Jocelyn: I was thinking that this hand [*left*] was addition and this hand [*right*] was subtraction.

Ms. Hazelton: So your left hand was going forward in this direction [*draws an arrow from left to right above the number line*]. **And that was addition? And your right was going in the other direction and that meant subtraction?**

Jocelyn: Uh-huh.

Ms. Hazelton: The direction that you go in on a number line, is that a way to think about subtraction? Subtraction feels like coming backward on a number line and addition feels like going forward?

Krista: It's sort of like my brother. He had homework for math and he had 32 soccer balls and 7 were taken away. And my dad told him, think what it equals, 7 plus something equals 32.

Ms. Hazelton: So Ben says that subtraction is the opposite of addition and addition is the opposite of subtraction. Jocelyn pictures things happening on the number line. I'm curious how people came up with ways to make the number 4.

Connor [*describing how he came up with 5 minus 1*]**:** I counted out 4 of the cubes. Then I just put 1 on with the cubes. Then I had 5. Then I took away 1.

Ms. Hazelton: You started out with 4 cubes because that was what you wanted to end up with and then you added on 1 more to get to 5? Could someone repeat Connor's strategy? What was Connor doing?

Sean: He's like counting on 1. He's counting on from the number he needed to get to. Then he just took away that 1.

Ms. Hazelton: Could someone repeat what Sean just said?

> *The room becomes very quiet. Some students yawn, a sign that it is getting hard for them to stay engaged. I decide to stay with it a bit longer to see if we can give Connor's idea a foothold so that we can come back to it the following day.*

Ms. Hazelton: I know that this is hard to think about. Would you like to hear Sean again? [*There is a murmur of willingness to listen some more.*] **Sean, try it again and this time use some cubes to show us what Connor is thinking.**

Sean: Well, Connor said if you were trying to get to 4 and you counted on 1, you would get 5 cubes and then you could just take off the one that you added on. [*As he speaks, Sean demonstrates adding on and removing 1 cube.*]

Claude: I think what he's saying is up there [*pointing to the number line representation*]. It would be like you go up 1 more from 4 and then you go backwards.

Ms. Hazelton: So if the number you wanted to make was 4 . . .

Claude: Like 4 plus 1 equals 5 and 5 take away 1 equals 4.

Ms. Hazelton: Could we try that idea with a different number?

Claude: We could do it with 7 and 8.

Ms. Hazelton: Could we show that with cubes? How many cubes would you like to start with?

Claude: Like, 7. [*Claude counts out 7 cubes.*] Then you would add on 1. Then that would equal 8.

Ms. Hazelton: How would you write the expression?

Claude: 7 plus 1 equals 8. So you would write 8 take away 1.

Ben: Well, I'm looking on the number line and I'm thinking 4 plus 5 equals 9 and 9 plus 5 equals . . . Oh, now I understand.

Ms. Hazelton: What were you thinking?

Ben: I was thinking that 4 plus 5 equals 9 and 9 plus 5 equals 4. But I was thinking of the wrong thing.

Ms. Hazelton: Are you saying to start with 4?

Ben: Uh-huh.

Ms. Hazelton: Then add on 5 and that will bring us to 9 [draws the jumps from 4 to 9].

Ben: And then I was thinking about addition, but it was supposed to be about subtraction.

The class discussion is prompted by puzzlement about how to generate an expression that results in a given difference. Young students—first and second graders—typically understand what is meant when they are asked to generate some numbers that, when added together, result in a certain *sum*, but can find it difficult to do the same with subtraction. The numbers in an addition expression all function in the same way—each is part of what is being accumulated to get the total amount. Young students usually do not have difficulty visualizing accumulation—start with an amount, then add on more. Visualizing subtraction is more complex—start with an amount, then remove part of that amount, and you are left with another part. Operating with a whole and a part of that whole is more difficult than putting together parts. When students are introduced to problems in which the difference is given and they are to come up with numbers that result in that difference, they are often stymied at first about how to get started.

After noting your thoughts on the contributions of Sean, Ben, Jocelyn, and Claude to the mathematical ideas being developed in the class discussion, read the following descriptions. Keep in mind that Ms. Hazelton knows her students over time and across different situations. Do characteristics she describes show up in the classroom episode you just read? Does any of what she says surprise you?

Sean has a strong understanding of numbers and number relationships. He regularly uses numerical reasoning when solving addition problems. Sometimes he struggles with explaining his thinking.

Ben's first language is not English. His grammar sounds awkward sometimes, but he is always fully engaged in math conversations. Ben is quick with numbers and often uses procedures that he's learned at home. He is reluctant to create models, preferring to stick with written numerals. Ben has a lot of number knowledge that appears to come from home. I'm not sure about the depth of understanding that is connected to that knowledge.

Math does not come to Jocelyn easily or automatically. She needs to work for what she learns. She is sometimes uncertain about drawing conclusions from what she's done. Jocelyn is most often engaged and trying to make sense of the ideas in whole-group discussions. She's willing to try to put words to what she and/or her classmates are noticing about the mathematics. Even when she struggles for the right words, she has the ability to talk in ways that invite her classmates to listen.

Claude is a quiet student who often appears to be disengaged during whole-group discussions. I wonder if he struggles to make sense of the ideas in our conversations. I'm not sure if he stops listening when it gets too hard or if there's something else that makes it hard for him to stay engaged. I frequently remind him to look at the person who's talking, particularly when they're demonstrating their thinking with cubes.

Look back at the discussion. What does each student contribute? Ben starts out with a broad statement, "I just know that subtraction is backward addition and addition is backward subtraction," which might lead us to believe that he has a firm grasp of this relationship. However, as the conversation proceeds, he needs to use a specific example and the number line to sort out for himself how this relationship actually works.

Sean introduces the idea that counting forward adds on and counting backward takes away. Building on Connor's example, Sean demonstrates with cubes that if you start with the desired difference (4, in his example), you can add on some amount (1, in his example). If you then start with that total (5) and subtract the same amount (1), you have a subtraction expression equivalent to that difference (5 − 1). By listening to Connor, Sean is able to refine and articulate his original idea. Sean notices a relationship between addition and subtraction that we could write more formally in this way: if $a + b = c$, then $c − b = a$.

Jocelyn offers gestures connected to her mental image that subtraction is "the opposite from addition." This leads to the drawing of a number line. Claude is then able to connect the number line representation to what Sean has demonstrated with cubes, "Like 4 plus 1 equals 5 and 5 take away 1 equals 4." He also applies his idea about subtraction being the opposite of addition to another set of numbers.

All four students contribute something important to the discussion. In this scenario, a wide range of students is participating in a high-level discussion of the relationship between addition and subtraction. They are making arguments and offering images and examples to explain and justify their ideas. Students are working through confusions by hearing and building on each others' ideas.

If we assessed these students on their answers to written addition and subtraction problems, we would see one aspect of their understanding and competence. Observing how they engage in reasoning about general claims gives a more rounded and complex picture. For example, Ben is quick with numbers and procedures and easily solves written problems, but does his focus on written numerals and reluctance to create models hold him back from other aspects of mathematical thinking? When Claude is disengaged and quiet, he could be seen as uninterested or confused, but with support from his teacher to attend to the conversation, he makes an important contribution, extending Sean's model to show it can represent other subtraction expressions.

EPISODE B: "HOW DID THE NUMERATOR GET TO THE DENOMINATOR?"

Marie Taft gives an account of a discussion in her fifth-grade class. Pay attention to both the teacher's instructional moves and to individual students' contributions. We join the class as they discuss how to tell when a fraction is equivalent to ½.

··

Steve: Fractions equal one half when they can be split down the middle.

Ms. Taft: Can you tell me more about that?

Steve: Yes, when they are shared equally, that is like splitting it right down the middle.

Kevin: What I think he means is that any time the numerator is half of the denominator, the fraction is equivalent to one-half.

Ms. Taft: Is there a clear and concise way I can record that?

Kevin: I know if the numerator is times 2 and you get the denominator, then the fraction equals one-half.

Ms. Taft: Is there a way I can record that without using so many words?

Lynne: You can say the numerator is the letter n and the denominator equals the letter d. Then you can write: if n times 2 equals d, then the fraction equals one-half.

Ms. Taft: Will that always be true? Can we apply this idea to other fractions we know?

Eddie: You can do this with any numerator and denominator. You just ask yourself, "How did the numerator get to the denominator?"

Ms. Taft: So, if we think about $\frac{9}{27}$ and I ask myself how does 9 get to 27? What would you answer? Talk about this idea with your partners.

Kevin [after some time passes during which students talk in pairs]: I know that 9 times 3 equals 27 and 27 divided by 3 equals 9, so I think that fraction equals one-third.

Ms. Taft: Ok, I am a little bit convinced. Can you convince me some more?

Steven: If you draw a rectangle and split it into thirds and color in one of the thirds, I can convince you. [I follow Steven's directions as shown below.]

Steven: Now, take those thirds and split them into 9 equal pieces each. You now have 27 pieces and you'll see 9 are shaded in, the same pieces that were shaded in when you drew one-third. [Note the changes in the following figure.]

At this point, many students want to share. I choose Lucy purposefully because she has been reserved since the beginning of the lesson.

Lucy: I know the same thing will work with one-fourth and three-twelfths. 1 times 4 is 4 and 3 times 4 is 12, so they both equal one-fourth. You can draw it the same way you did with Steven's one-third and ³⁄₂₇. [The following image applies Lucy's idea to show ¼ = ³⁄₁₂.]

The group tests a few more ideas for ¼ and ⅕.

Ms. Taft: Is there a way I can write these ideas in a quicker way?

Steven: If you do numerator times 2 equals denominator to get one-half, all you have to do is numerator times any number to get one-any numberth. Like ¹⁰⁄₁₀₀ is ¹⁄₁₀. ⁵⁄₂₀ is ¼. It's hard to write one rule for all of these examples, but I know it will work.

At this point, I feel like it is a good place to stop. The students are coming up with some pretty big ideas, but time is getting away from us and I do not want to exhaust them. When we get back together, I would like to continue testing out their ideas and writing more concise ways to summarize the concepts they are working with.

....

Many students add important comments to this discussion. Before reading further, look back at Eddie and Lucy's comments. What do they contribute to the discussion?

Eddie and Lucy both extend ideas others have brought up. Eddie realizes that one must think about the relationship between the numerator and denominator to find equivalent fractions. His question, "How did the numerator get to the denominator?" can be paraphrased as, "What can you multiply the numerator by to get the denominator?" Lucy is carefully following Steven's representation and argues that a version of his image can also show that $\frac{1}{4} = \frac{3}{12}$. Both Eddie and Lucy are making connections among individual examples to develop general ideas about equivalent fractions.

But look at how differently Ms. Taft describes them:

Eddie is generally pretty advanced in his thinking. He is often quick to do computation accurately and can be much more efficient than me at times. However, he is known to rush through things because he knows that math is easy for him.

Lucy seems to be most efficient and accurate when she has explicit steps to follow. However, she tends not to meet success when she is asked to think for herself or read a problem for meaning.

A few weeks later, the teacher interviews Eddie and Lucy individually, asking them to look at pairs of expressions and decide whether one of the expressions is greater than the other or the two expressions are equal. She asks them to try to compare the expressions without carrying out the indicated operations. Determining what you know about a problem before trying to solve it is something that the class has been doing routinely throughout the year.

The first pair of expressions is $125 + 75$ and $175 + 25$. Eddie says, "You could change the numbers so they are the same. They're both 100 plus 25 plus 75, just switched around. In addition, it doesn't matter if you change the order of the numbers." Eddie appears to understand that numbers in an addition expression can be taken apart and put back together in any order without changing the sum. Eddie seems confident in applying what he understands.

Lucy, on the other hand, does not have this confidence. Even for this straightforward addition problem, she carries out the computation to determine if the two expressions are equivalent. She says, "I am going to pretend that 75 is under 125 [that is, written as a vertical problem] and get 190 plus 10 to get 200. The second one [175 + 25] is going to be 200, too, because if I put it underneath [she writes it vertically]. . . . they are the same."

$$
\begin{array}{r}
125 \\
75 \\
\hline
190 \\
10 \\
\hline
200
\end{array}
\qquad\qquad
\begin{array}{r}
175 \\
25 \\
\hline
200
\end{array}
$$

At this point in the interview, Ms. Taft is listening to how Lucy responds in order to get a fuller picture of how Lucy approaches these problems.

When Eddie is asked to compare 300 ÷ 15 and 300 ÷ 30, he reasons, "300 divided by 15 is greater because you are dividing by a lower number, so you will have a greater amount. The more you divide, the less you get. If that was pieces of pizza, 15 people would get more, 30 people would get less." Faced with the same comparison, Lucy first tries to carry out the computation, but now Ms. Taft decides to intervene. She suggests that Lucy use a story context, which prompts Lucy to develop the following: "There are 300 kids in the schoolyard. I want to split them into groups. How many will be in each group? . . . 300 divided by 15 will have bigger groups because they have a smaller number of groups." To see if Lucy can continue to apply this reasoning, Ms. Taft presents another division problem, and the following exchange takes place:

....

$$500 \div 20 \qquad 500 \div 40$$

Lucy: 5 times 4 equals 20 . . .

Ms. Taft: Please don't try to solve it.

Lucy: 500 divided by 20 will be greater because 20 groups will have more in each group if you think about the schoolyard story.

....

The situation is different when the teacher asks them to compare 125 × 75 and 175 × 25. Before you read on, decide whether these two multiplication expressions are equivalent. See if you can develop a representation that would convince someone else.

Eddie's response is: "These would also be the same because it is just like the first one [the two addition expressions]." Ms. Taft asks him to estimate the product for 125 × 75. Eddie says, "Between 7,000 and 8,000 because 100 times 70 equals 7,000, so it has to be more than that." When she asks him about the second expression, he responds, "It would be the same." Eddie insists that the two expressions are equivalent without estimating the product of 175 × 25 or thinking through how the two expressions could be broken down. (One way to break apart the two expressions is:

$125 \times 75 = (100 \times 75) + (25 \times 75)$, and $175 \times 25 = (100 \times 25) + (75 \times 25)$. The product of 25 and 75 appears in both, but 100×75 is considerably greater than 100×25, so 125×75 is greater than 175×25.)

Lucy, with some support from Ms. Taft, *does* apply knowledge about the properties of multiplication in her reasoning:

....

Lucy: I think the first group of numbers [125 × 75] is greater.

Ms. Taft: Can you prove it to me?

Lucy: Yes, by doing it traditionally.

Ms. Taft: Can you prove it to me without solving it? Can you think of a story to go with it?

Lucy: 125 boxes with 75 clementines in each. How many clementines are there in all? If I do 75 times 100, I will get 7,500. If I do 25 times 100, then I will get 2,500. So I think the first group will be greater because 7,500 is greater than 2,500.

....

In this exchange, the teacher suggests that Lucy develop a story context to help her think through the problem. When she does this, we see that she is able to apply the distributive property, breaking up the two expressions in order to compare them.

IN CONCLUSION . . .

It might be argued that students having difficulty with computation should master procedures first before attempting to make generalizations. At the other end of the spectrum, students who can solve most computation problems easily might seem to have little more to learn about the operations. Our accounts of Eddie and Lucy argue otherwise.

Both students benefit from comparing expressions to determine if one is greater without carrying out the computation. Eddie is learning to develop mathematical arguments, such as the one he gives for the comparison of $300 \div 15$ and $300 \div 30$. He contributes to class discussions by articulating generalizations, as he does when he suggests that their ideas about fractions equivalent to ½ can be extended and modified to apply to other fractions. But Eddie can make incorrect judgments when he does not stop for long enough to think through the problem and sort out the properties of the operation.

Lucy will continue to develop reasoning based on story contexts and representations. This will help her develop arguments about numbers and operations that do not rely on computing each individual answer. Lucy's contributions indicate that she has made important steps in this direction, although she needs to develop confidence in her ability to reason without computing first.

In this chapter, we have seen a wide range of students growing in their mathematical understanding as they focus on articulating, representing, and justifying general claims about mathematical operations. In later chapters, we will continue to argue that this focus on the operations themselves is basic for *all* students to develop computational competence in a way that will eventually support their understanding of algebra. Keep in mind the range of students with which you work as you read the next two chapters. In these chapters, you will learn more about how students articulate, represent, and prove general claims, how to incorporate this work into classroom instruction, and why this work is important. Then, in Chapter 6, we will return to specific examples of students with different learning needs and how their teachers support them to build their knowledge of the operations. ■

FOCUS QUESTIONS

GENERALIZING IN ARITHMETIC WITH A RANGE OF LEARNERS

1. **In Chapter 3, Episode A is an extended narrative from a second-grade class.**

   - Identify and describe the mathematics that the students are grappling with at the beginning of the episode. Why might the students find this math idea confusing? What kinds of math tasks provide a means to work on this idea?

   - Follow through the mathematics as the case unfolds: What is it that Ben and Sean offer in the first section? What does Jocelyn contribute? What does Connor add to the discussion? What does Claude contribute?

   - After the case, the teacher offers brief descriptions of four students: Sean, Ben, Jocelyn, and Claude. In what ways do those descriptions match the sense of each student you got from reading the case? In what ways were those descriptions at variance with your expectations? What questions does this raise about your own students?

2. **In Chapter 3, Episode B is an extended narrative from a fifth-grade class.**

   - Identify and describe the mathematics that the students are working on at the beginning of the case (Steve, Kevin). What kinds of math tasks provide a means to work on this idea?

   - Follow through the mathematics as the case unfolds: What does Eddie add on early in the discussion? What is Steven's contribution as the discussion continues? What does Lucy contribute near the end of the case?

   - The teacher offers brief descriptions of two students, Eddie and Lucy. In what ways do those descriptions match the sense of each student you got from reading the case? In what ways were those descriptions at variance with your expectations? What questions does this raise about your own students?

   - The chapter continues with portions of interviews with Eddie and Lucy. Identify the math ideas that underlie the tasks these students are working on. What do you learn about Lucy by examining her thinking? What do you learn about Eddie by examining his thinking?

3. The title of Chapter 3 includes the phrase, "Range of Learners." What questions, comments, or new ideas about the meaning of that phrase have been highlighted by the examples in this chapter? What questions does this raise for you about your own students?

Articulating General Claims

So far you have read about engaging elementary students in noticing patterns in the operations and studied examples of students noticing and acting on generalizations as they do arithmetic. We have also identified instructional moves teachers can use to help students develop mathematical reasoning. Next we examine how to help students articulate general mathematical statements.

An episode from a class exploring equivalent multiplication expressions provides an example of the sort of patterns students notice and the generalizations they can make. Fifth-grade teacher Adio Kweku has asked her students to describe what they notice about the equations $4 \times 10 = 8 \times 5$ and $26 \times 12 = 13 \times 24$. Examine the statements of two students:

....

Amania: It is the same product because they are equivalent. If you double one factor and halve the other, it will result in the same product because it will stay the same product and not a wrong product.

Sherry: When you double one number and you halve the other, the result is the same product because they are equivalents, or the other way to say it is that they are in the same family.

....

Amania and Sherry are working to articulate a general claim: If one factor of a multiplication expression is multiplied by 2 and the other factor is divided by 2, the product remains the same. Although the students are still learning to articulate a claim succinctly, their statements include the essential elements: the claim is about multiplication (implied by the use of the terms *factor* and *product*), one factor is halved and the other is doubled, and the product remains the same.

Articulating general claims is essential to investigating generalizations. As students put their ideas into words, they clarify their ideas, develop common language, and come to a common understanding of exactly what their general claim is. Once they have agreed what it is they are trying to prove, they can work together to justify their claim.

Careful articulation of general claims helps prevent overgeneralization. For example, if students simply say "doubling and halving" to describe the idea Amania and Sherry are working on without spelling out that their claim is about multiplication, other students might assume the generalization applies to *any* expression. For example, they might think, incorrectly, that $26 + 12 = 13 + 24$. In this equation, *addends* have been doubled and halved instead of *factors*.

Articulating general claims is challenging, but worth the effort. In this chapter, we will look at several classrooms engaged in this process in order to highlight students' efforts and teachers' strategies.

ARTICULATING A PROPERTY OF ADDITION IN GRADE 1

From an early age, students notice and are interested in consistent features of the operations, although they may not yet have the ability to articulate them. Even as these students are just learning to count, compute, and use arithmetic symbols, teachers can ask them to explain their thinking to help them develop language for generalizations.

Robert Williams' students are examining the relationship between the equations $3 + 6 = 9$ and $6 + 3 = 9$. Students each have twenty cubes to model the equations. They work with partners to talk over any relationships they notice. Mr. Williams moves from pair to pair to discuss their ideas. Notice the language the students use to express their thinking.

Mr. Williams: What are you noticing about the number sentences?

Chris: You are using the same numbers every time. 3 plus 6 equals 9, 6 plus 3 equals 9. It is the same number sentence.

Mr. Williams: Why do you say it is the same one?

Chris: This right here [*pointing to $3 + 6 = 9$*] is the opposite of this [*pointing to $6 + 3 = 9$*].

Mr. Williams: Hmm. What do you mean it is the opposite?

Chris: I mean that it's the same but the other way around.

Mr. Williams: Ted, what are you noticing?

Ted: 3 plus 6 is 9 and 6 plus 3 is 9. It is the same number sentence but backward.

Chris first calls $3 + 6 = 9$ and $6 + 3 = 9$ the "same number sentence" and then refines his idea by using the term *opposite*. Upon questioning from Mr. Williams, Chris defines what he means by *opposite*: "It's the same but the other way around." Ted expresses the same idea by saying the number sentences are the same but "backward." Mr. Williams' questions require the first graders to describe and clarify their observations and their thinking.

As the lesson continues, Mr. Williams asks another student, Ethan, who is also talking about the two addition sentences as "opposites," to demonstrate for the whole class what he means. Ethan separates a stack of 9 cubes into a stack of 3 and a stack of 6. By changing which stack is in which hand, the same cubes become a stack of 6 and a stack of 3. Since none of the cubes are removed and no other cubes are added, the total remains the same.

Mr. Williams then asks his students to consider whether this holds true for other numbers, and has them consider $7 + 3 = 10$ and $3 + 7 = 10$. After a short time for students to examine these equations in pairs, Mr. Williams brings them together for another class discussion. He wants to highlight the idea that their notion of "opposites" is a general property of addition, but not subtraction.

Mr. Williams: Let's review what we said. You said that 3 plus 7 is the same as 7 plus 3 except that it is the opposite. The numbers are switched. Now, does the opposite work for all the sentences? What about 10 minus 3 equals 7? If I switch the numbers around, does it work with 3 minus 10 equals 7?

There is a chorus of "no!"

Mr. Williams: So when does this idea of opposites work? . . . Does "opposites" work with addition and subtraction? Let's write a rule for when we can use the "opposite" rule.

Peter: You can use the "opposite" rule when we have a plus sign.

Mr. Williams writes Peter's rule on the board and asks the class to read it.

Mr. Williams: Does this mean, when we are adding?

Peter: Yes.

Mr. Williams: Let's test out Peter's rule to see if it works. Talk to your neighbor about a number sentence using small numbers. *[Partners talk.]* Who can give me some new, small numbers that would work?

Yvette: 2 plus 1 equals 3.

Mr. Williams: So now, who can apply Peter's rule? How can we use the opposite rule?

Hal: 1 plus 2 equals 3.

Mr. Williams: Does Peter's rule work?

Class: Yes.

Mr. Williams elicits another example and its opposite: $2 + 4 = 6$, $4 + 2 = 6$.

Mr. Williams: Let's test our rule. Is this a number sentence with a plus sign?

Class: Yes.

Mr. Williams: Did the numbers switch places?

Class: Yes.

Mr. Williams: Will the opposite always give us the same number?

Some students respond "yes," while others say "no."

Elizabeth: When you have take-away. When you have take-away it doesn't equal the same. If I did 6 take away 1 equals 5 and 1 take away 6 equals 0.[1]

Those students who say "yes" are thinking in terms of Peter's statement, that the opposite rule applies to addition. Elizabeth says "no," and explains that Peter's opposites rule does not apply to subtraction.

Mr. Williams and his class are working to develop shared language for a property they have noticed about addition (the commutative property of addition). They use the term *opposites* to name this property and illustrate it with cubes. Students specify that this rule applies only to addition, not subtraction.

Although students articulate general claims during this classroom episode, it is important to note that the work of making sense of such claims is not accomplished in a single lesson. Although Ethan offered a demonstration, other students may still need to think through how the action with the cubes relates to the symbols on the

1   This is a common response in the primary grades. Elizabeth and her classmates will eventually learn that $1 - 6 = -5$. For now, in first grade, the important point for them to recognize is that $1 - 6$ does not produce the same result as $6 - 1$.

page. Furthermore, it is uncertain whether students understand that Peter's opposites rule applies to all numbers. They are probably thinking about numbers with which they are most familiar, numbers from 1 to 10 or 20. What if Mr. Williams were to ask them about numbers just beyond their familiarity? Will the rule still work if you switch the addends in 48 + 37? What about 593 + 638? We will return to the question of how students demonstrate their understanding when we discuss proof in Chapters 5 and 8.

As students encounter new kinds of numbers, there will be still more questions to consider: Does the commutative property also hold for fractions? Does it hold for integers? It takes years for students to fully absorb even such a basic idea as the commutative property of addition, though they may initially encounter it as early as first grade.

ARTICULATING IDEAS ABOUT EQUIVALENT SUBTRACTION EXPRESSIONS IN GRADE 3

Alice Kaye's third graders have already spent time discussing this generalization: In an addition expression, if one addend decreases by some amount and the other addend increases by that same amount, the sum remains the same. Now that they are working on subtraction, Ms. Kaye decides that her students are ready to encounter the following generalization: In a subtraction expression, if both numbers are increased by the same amount, the difference remains the same.

The lesson is presented in three sections. Pay particular attention to Ms. Kaye's moves: how she organizes the lesson, how she responds to her students' thinking, and how she supports and challenges them to articulate the generalization.

Helping Students Notice a Consistent Feature

In the previous lesson, the class considered a sequence of equations with small numbers: $5 - 3 = 2$, $6 - 4 = 2$, $7 - 5 = 2$, and $8 - 6 = 2$. They created story problems for the equations. Today, Ms. Kaye begins by asking for subtraction expressions equal to 25. Nancy offers $26 - 1$; Helen, $27 - 2$. In response to Ms. Kaye's request for a story situation, Todd suggests, "I had 26 baseball cards and my little brother stole 1."

As the class continues creating subtraction expressions equal to 25, they soon have this list:

$$25 - 0 = 25$$
$$26 - 1 = 25$$
$$27 - 2 = 25$$
$$28 - 3 = 25$$
$$29 - 4 = 25$$
$$30 - 5 = 25$$
$$31 - 6 = 25$$

Nora: I noticed something. I thought it was going to go like . . . Since this one *[the column of quantities being subtracted]* went 0, 1, 2, 3, 4, 5, 6, I thought this one *[the column of starting quantities]* was going to go 25, 24, 23, 22. . . .

Matt: That's what I thought, too.

....

Nora and Matt are drawing on work done earlier on sequences of addition equations. Ms. Kaye posts a list of the addition equations Nora and Matt have in mind next to the first list.

$25 - 0 = 25$	$25 + 0 = 25$
$26 - 1 = 25$	$24 + 1 = 25$
$27 - 2 = 25$	$23 + 2 = 25$
$28 - 3 = 25$	$22 + 3 = 25$
$29 - 4 = 25$	$21 + 4 = 25$
$30 - 5 = 25$	$20 + 5 = 25$
$31 - 6 = 25$	$19 + 6 = 25$

After looking at the lists, Nora says, "So, I guess it only works with adding, not subtracting."

Notice what Ms. Kaye is doing. She has in mind a generalization she believes her students are ready to encounter and has allocated several days for them to consider it. First, they worked with smaller numbers, and now they move onto larger numbers. On both days, she asks for story contexts to help represent the actions implied by the operation. Once the list of equations is on the board, Ms. Kaye invites students to comment. When Nora and Matt say they had expected a different pattern to emerge, Ms. Kaye then puts up a sequence of addition equations related to Nora and Matt's expectations for the class to compare to the first list. She acknowledges her students' expectation and brings their attention to differences between the operations.

Challenging Students to Verbalize What They Notice: What's the It?

Once students notice a pattern, it is important they learn to articulate what they see. When Nora says, "I guess it only works with adding, not subtracting," she has noticed something significant. However, if the class continues to talk about the pattern as *it*, there is no assurance that they are all talking about the same idea.

In the next part of this lesson, Ms. Kaye is persistent in asking her students to put their generalization into words.

....

Ms. Kaye: What only works with adding? What's the *it*?

Nora: The . . . um . . . the . . . the. . . . .

The class waits, but Nora cannot put words to what she is thinking.

Carl: There's both the same thing in the middle—0, 1, 2, 3, 4, 5, 6 *[pointing to the subtraction sequence]* and 0, 1, 2, 3, 4, 5, 6 *[pointing to the addition sequence]*. But 25 26, 27, 28, 29, 30 is the other way from 25, 24, 23, 22, 21, 20, 19.

Clarissa: I noticed that's because it's going down *[pointing to the first column in the addition sequence]*, and this is going up *[pointing to the first column in the subtraction sequence]*. Because in order to minus, you usually have to go up, because if you did like 25 minus 0 equals 25, 24 minus 1 would be 23. That would be if you did the same thing as this *[pointing to the addition sequence]*.

Ms. Kaye: And what's the *this* you're talking about?

Clarissa: 25 plus 0, 24 plus 1, 23 plus 2. Because that would be adding 1 on, but you're subtracting 1 off.

Note that Clarissa is close to specifying the generalization about addition that the class had discussed previously. In response to Clarissa's comments, Ms. Kaye records another string of equations, so the class chart now looks like this:

25 − 0 = 25	25 − 0 = 25	25 + 0 = 25
26 − 1 = 25	24 − 1 = 23	24 + 1 = 25
27 − 2 = 25	23 − 2 = 21	23 + 2 = 25
28 − 3 = 25	22 − 3 = 19	22 + 3 = 25
29 − 4 = 25		21 + 4 = 25
30 − 5 = 25		20 + 5 = 25
31 − 6 = 25		19 + 6 = 25

Todd: Since this one is going down *[pointing to the first addend in the addition sequence]*, this one *[pointing to the second addend in the addition sequence]* has to go up.

Several students have now pointed out different patterns in the sequences: which columns are increasing and which are decreasing. But Ms. Kaye continues to push.

Ms. Kaye: What's the idea about addition and subtraction that's being revealed here?

Jonah: I think the reason that both of these columns [*in the first subtraction sequence*] are going up in value is because if you want to get the same thing, if you have a higher number to minus, you need a higher number to minus it to 25. But if you have a lower number to start with, you don't need as many numbers to get to 25.

Many students: Ohhhh! I get it!

....

Notice that Ms. Kaye repeatedly presses students to articulate what they notice, not accepting such phrases as, "It works. . . ." without further clarification. For example, she asks "What only works with adding? What's the *it?*" Jonah eventually articulates an idea his classmates understand.

The class has time to work at articulating their observations. There are long pauses, and students stumble with the language. When a student mentions a third sequence of equations, Ms. Kaye adds the new list to the board, keeping the lists organized and readable so that students can compare. She encourages the students to look at the pattern of numbers in each column—when they go up and when they go down—realizing that this is a step toward deeper understanding.

Although noticing the patterns in the columns of numbers is significant, students still need to relate those patterns to the behavior of the operations. Ms. Kaye poses a question to take the class to the next level: "What's the idea about addition and subtraction that's being revealed here?" Ms. Kaye is asking the class to take a broader view, and Jonah responds by talking about the action of subtraction.

Providing Opportunity for More Students to Verbalize

Jonah has moved the class forward with his claim about subtraction. Although many students respond by saying that they get it, there is more work to do. They continue to work to clarify the idea and develop a more concise articulation. Ms. Kaye suggests that Jonah turn back to the story context offered in the beginning of the lesson.

....

Ms. Kaye: So can you use Todd's example to talk us through your idea? Todd's talking about always wanting to make sure he has 25 cards. Can you use that?

Jonah: If he starts with more, his brother has to take more to get to 25, because there's more cards to take.

Frannie: It sounds simple, but it really isn't.

Manuel: It's just like . . . he has a bigger number here. So he has to take away more in order to get to the number he wants to get.

Sierra: Yeah, we knew that, and we thought everyone knew that, but now we just sort of figured it out.

Helen: Knew what?

Ms. Kaye: What is the idea, Sierra?

Sierra: The idea is that you need more to take away and get the same amount. If I had 26 and I minus 1, if you want the. . . . That would be the same as . . . if you wanted to have the same answer, and you could start with 27 and take away 2.

Addison: The reason why they're both going up is, since it's higher, then you have to subtract more to get to that, but if it's less, you don't need as much to get to that number. It's less numbers to get to it.

Elizabeth: I think I know why this column [of starting amounts] is going up. Because these [the differences] are the same, and in order to make the subtraction equal 25, each number [the starting amount] you have to go higher and higher. And in this [the addition sequence], each number, you can go lower because you're adding. You're taking it apart on one number and putting it on the other.

....

Ms. Kaye has her students pair up and asks, "To get the same answer in subtraction, what do you have to do? Turn and talk about the ideas we have been thinking about during this discussion." After a few minutes, she asks students to write down their ideas individually. This allows all students time to work at articulating the idea.

Ms. Kaye reports: "The results were very mixed, from students who could only write about addition, to those who were noticing some regularity in the sequence of subtraction equations and were trying to put the idea into words."

Ms. Kaye recognizes that stating an idea in one's own words is different from understanding someone else's statement. Furthermore, stating an idea in writing is different from stating it orally. She gives her students time to engage in each of these activities.

Note that Ms. Kaye herself could have stated the idea for her students to recite back to her. There may be times when a teacher chooses to provide an example of concise language for students to consider. However, Ms. Kaye recognizes the value to her students of finding the language to express a mathematical idea for themselves. The idea is developed and clarified as students take up the challenge of articulating it.

ARTICULATING IDEAS ABOUT ADDITION IN GRADE 7

Nadia Thompson is introducing a new routine to her seventh graders. Students are given a mathematical sentence and asked to explain how they know it is true or false without computing. Ms. Thompson writes on the board:

Do not solve. Is the following number sentence true or false? How can you show it without solving? 24 + 26 = 25 + 25

Students think individually and then talk to a partner. When they come back together in the whole group, all responses are based on calculations: Both sides equal 50 and so they are the same. Ms. Thompson reminds the class of the directions and asks, "How can you show it without solving?"

Students are still unsure about what they are being asked to do. Ms. Thompson revises her question, asking students to generate other sentences like the original. The class offers three:

$$13 + 17 = 11 + 19 \quad 27 + 13 = 24 + 16 \quad 7 + 16 = 10 + 13$$

....

Ms. Thompson: Now that we have four number sentences, tell me what patterns you see.

Mason: We keep subtracting from one number and adding it to the other to make the numbers the same.

Everett: No, the numbers aren't always the same.

Mason: See with 13 plus 17 equals 11 plus 19, we subtracted 2 from 17 and added 2 to 13 and that made them both 15. Then we did the same thing to 11 and 19. We subtracted 4 from 19 and we added it to 11. That makes 15 plus 15. Now we have 2 fifteens on both sides and that proves the sentence must have been true.

Everett: In the sentence, 7 plus 16 equals 10 plus 13, we subtract 3 from 16 and add it to the 7. Then we have 10 plus 13, and that was a different way of showing the sentence was true without adding all the numbers and not all of the numbers are the same.

....

Mason has shown how each expression can be transformed to 15 + 15:

$$13 + 17 = (13 + 2) + (17 - 2) = 15 + 15$$

$$11 + 19 = (11 + 4) + (19 - 4) = 15 + 15$$

Everett comments on Mason's method, explaining that equality between two expressions can be demonstrated without creating an expression where the two addends are the same.

Mason acknowledges that Everett's way of seeing the equations works, too. Students continue by demonstrating the transformation of one expression to the other using cubes. Eventually, they explain that their action with cubes can be applied to any set of addends.

No matter what the grade level, when students are asked for the first time to reason about relationships rather than perform a calculation, many students are not sure how to proceed. Ms. Thompson had anticipated that her seventh graders might say something like, "If you have an addition expression, add some amount to one addend and subtract that same amount from the other, and the total stays the same." Instead, even though the directions state not to solve, computing is students' first impulse. She finally gets them to generalize by asking them to generate number sentences like the original one. They communicate a sense of an underlying pattern, not in words, but by producing additional instances.

Through discussion and explaining their thinking to others, these students clarify for themselves and for others the consistent features they notice. They are now on the way to articulating a general claim.

WHAT TEACHERS DO TO SUPPORT ARTICULATION

Articulating general claims about the behavior of the operations is challenging and important. We have considered classroom episodes from grades 1 to 7 involving students engaged in this work. As early as first grade, students notice regularities in their calculations and consistencies across problems, and they take first steps toward describing them.

As students continue to study mathematics, they usually become more fluent with computation. However, without an instructional focus on generalizing integrated into their arithmetic instruction, they are unlikely to recognize and articulate the generalizations that underlie their computation methods. With this focus, students in the elementary grades can develop facility for stating general claims. For example, consider these generalizations written by Marlena Diaz's fifth graders after working on generalizations throughout the year:

> *We worked on doubling and halving, where if you have a multiplication problem and you double one number and halve the other, you will always end up with the same answer, because it won't take any away or add any.*

> *In addition, you can add 1 and subtract 1 to get the same thing (4 + 7 = 5 + 6), but in multiplication you don't (4 × 7 = 28 and 5 × 6 = 30) because you add one group of something and subtract a group of something else.*

The first statement is a claim about equivalent multiplication expressions. In the second, another student explains why a generalization about equivalent addition expressions does not apply to multiplication. This student uses specific numbers to illustrate the claim.

The classroom episodes in this chapter illustrate actions taken by teachers to help their students articulate general claims. These strategies and stances include:

- *Providing regular routines to set up habits for math explorations.* These routines include Alice Kaye's "Number of the Day" and Nadia Thompson's "Is the Number Sentence True?" See Chapter 2 for more about these routines.

- *Creating variations within routines to highlight various aspects of a claim or to call attention to an unstated assumption.* When Nadia Thompson's students are not sure how to explain without calculating that a given equation is true, she creates a variation of the routine. She asks that they come up with other equations that illustrate the same principle.

- *Giving students multiple opportunities to clarify for themselves the ideas they are working to express.* The routines provide time for students to develop their own ideas about consistencies and regularities they are noticing. For example, to move her students' thinking forward, Ms. Kaye's next lesson involved the following problem:

$$8 - 5 = 9 - \underline{}$$

Is the answer 4 or 6? How do you know?

This variation provides a different way for students to consider the same generalization about equivalent subtraction expressions.

- *Encouraging representations such as cubes, diagrams, drawings, and story contexts to provide tools for expressing ideas.* Robert Williams asks his students to use cubes to think about what happens when the addends of an addition expression are switched. Alice Kaye's students devise a story to help them think about the sequence of subtraction expressions. These representations help them talk about the patterns they recognize in the symbols.

- *Insisting that students explain what they mean by "it" or "this".* Alice Kaye consistently asks her students to explain what they mean when they say, "It works." Some students are even learning to ask this of each other; when Sierra says, "We knew that, and we thought everyone knew that, but now we just sort of figured it out," Helen responds, "Knew what?"

- *Giving many students the opportunity to state a claim in their own words and varying how they do this: individually or in pairs, orally or in writing.* In all the classes we've seen, students work together as a class to articulate and clarify generalizations. Alice Kaye asks her students to turn to a partner and state their understanding of the generalization under discussion. She then has the students write down their own version of the generalization. Similarly, Marlena Diaz requires her students to produce written descriptions of their findings.

- *Refining language and offering vocabulary as needed.* When first expressing their ideas, students need to use informal language. As their ideas take shape, mathematics vocabulary is introduced. For example, students learn to use *factor* or *addend* in place of *this number* or *that number*. In Adio Kweku's class, we saw students use the terms *factor* and *product* to state a claim about equivalent multiplication expressions.

IN CONCLUSION . . .

Learning to articulate one's ideas clearly is an important part of mathematics. Articulating a general claim involves answering questions such as "What does *it* mean?" "Is there a way we could say more clearly which number you are talking about?" or "For which operation is this statement true?" Articulation does not necessarily occur only after a complete formulation of a mathematical idea; rather, just as in writing a story or essay, ideas are clarified by trying out and revising wording. When students work together to articulate a general claim, they build on each other's ideas to come to a common understanding. In the next chapter, we will look at how students begin to justify their general claims. ■

FOCUS QUESTIONS

ARTICULATING GENERAL CLAIMS

1. Consider Mr. Williams' grade 1 classroom narrative in which he works with his class on noticing and articulating the commutative property of addition.

   • What do you notice about the questions that Mr. Williams asks?

   • What is the impact of his questions on his students?

   • What ideas about posing questions does this bring up for you as you consider your own teaching practice?

2. Consider the commutative property of addition for yourself. How many ways can you explain why $2 + 5 = 5 + 2$? Use number lines, story contexts, drawings, and a variety of representations.

3. In the grade 3 classroom narrative, Ms. Kaye's students identify number patterns as they look at sequences of arithmetic expressions. However, finding number patterns is not the end of the process.

   • What happens in this case, after the patterns have been noted?

   • What math ideas are the focus of the work and how are those ideas related to noticing patterns?

   • What questions does this raise about the math work you want your students to take on?

4. As Ms. Kaye's classroom discussion continues, the students call upon a story context to help them make sense of the subtraction claim they are working with. Consider this equation: $15 - 6 = 16 - 7$. How can you use story contexts, number lines, actions with cubes, and other representations to explain why it is true? How would your representations change if the equation was $34 - 16 = 35 - 17$?

5. The end of Chapter 4 includes a bulleted list of strategies teachers can use to help their students articulate general claims. Choose one or two you would like to incorporate into your work with students. What first steps might you take to do that?

5

Developing Mathematical Arguments
Representation-Based Proof

This chapter examines how students in the elementary grades develop arguments, or proofs,[1] that show why particular generalizations are true. The examples illustrate characteristics of student arguments, representational tools students use to create arguments, and ways in which teachers support such thinking in their students.

APPROACHES TO JUSTIFYING A GENERAL CLAIM

There are various ways we come to believe in the truth of a mathematical statement, depending on the context and on our background and experiences. In mathematics, among students and adults, four different approaches to justifying a general claim are typical:

1. Accepting the claim on authority

2. Trying it out with examples

---

1   The terms *argument* and *proof* are used as synonyms throughout this chapter. Similarly, the terms *general claim* and *generalization* are used as synonyms.

3. Applying mathematical reasoning based on a visual representation or story context

4. Proving using algebraic notation and the laws of arithmetic

As you read the discussion that follows, see if you can identify the different approaches that students use to justify their claims.

Jennifer Schmidt's fourth graders are working with the "What Do You Know About _____?" routine. This routine was introduced in Chapter 2 and helps develop reasoning about computation and about the nature of the operations. During this routine, students typically bring up a range of ideas. The teacher selects which ideas to examine as a class, depending on what content she wants to stress.

· ·

$$327 + 245 = ?$$

Ms. Schmidt: **What do you know about 327 plus 245? What can you say about the sum?**

Angela: It is more than 500.

Teri: And less than 600.

Mannie: I know it will be an even number.

Ms. Schmidt: **How do you know that?**

Audrey: The numbers are both odd and if you add two odd numbers, it will be even.

Ms. Schmidt: **Does everyone agree? Is that always true?**

· ·

Angela and Teri have made comments about estimating the sum of 327 and 245. However, Ms. Schmidt chooses to pursue Audrey's claim about adding odd numbers. She asks, "Is that always true?" to engage her students in the core mathematical process of making a mathematical argument.

· ·

Fiona: My teacher told us that last year. An odd plus an odd is even.

Samantha: Look. 7 plus 5 equals 12; 5 plus 3 equals 8; 17 plus 7 equals 24. It just is.

Ms. Schmidt: **But Audrey is saying this works for *all* pairs of odd numbers, right?**

Audrey: Yes. It doesn't matter what the numbers are.

Joshua: But there are lots and lots of numbers. I don't think you can ever be sure.

Ms. Schmidt: I hear Audrey saying that *every* time you add two odd numbers, you get an even number. Joshua is saying, if you haven't tried all the numbers, how can you be sure?

Mannie: It has to be that way. We all know that.

Ms. Schmidt: What does Audrey mean that it doesn't matter what the numbers are? Can you think of a way to show how that can be true? We have been using stories or cubes to make arguments. Take a few minutes, talk to your partner, and see how stories or cubes might help you.

Ms. Schmidt [*after a few minutes*]**: I heard Mannie's group use a story. Would you share?**

Mannie: It's like you have some people in one class and everyone has a work partner except one person. Then you have another class and it is the same; everyone has a partner except one person. If you put the two classes together, everyone stays with his or her partner and then the ones without partners pair up. When the two classes are together, everyone has a partner. That would make it even.

Audrey: I can show it with cubes. These are both odd numbers. Every cube is paired up except one. I don't even need to know what the number is. If every cube is paired except the one at the end, then it's odd. When I put them together, the two end ones pair up. That makes the total even.

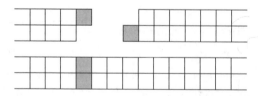

....

This discussion includes examples of three types of justification.

- *Accepting the claim on authority.* Fiona calls upon the authority of a previous teacher to justify the rule that the sum of two odd numbers is even. In life, we often turn to authorities to provide us with information and guidance. Part of learning to make good decisions is learning how to choose and evaluate which authorities we are going to trust. In mathematics, there may be times when we refer to an authority for an answer. We might forget the definition of a scalene triangle and refer to a text or ask someone we know who has the right expertise.

However, accepting a mathematical claim on authority does not help students make sense of the situation for themselves, nor does it add to their understanding of the operations or the structure of the number system. Referring to an authority for justification may indicate that the student does not yet know that proving a claim is even a possibility.

- *Trying it out with examples.* Samantha produces a set of examples to justify the claim. Because her claim is true for several examples, she concludes, "It just is." Generating examples as a means of justification is a typical response when elementary students are asked how they know a statement is *always* true. Creating a set of examples can be a useful step in making a mathematical argument. It is a way to develop a sense of whether the statement is true for different kinds of numbers. Through examining examples, we also start to see mathematical relationships and structure that can lead to insight into why the consistencies we are seeing occur. However, a set of examples does not constitute an argument that a claim applies to an infinite class of numbers. For example, consider this statement: The sum of any two prime numbers is even. It is possible to generate a long list of pairs of prime numbers with an even sum: $5 + 7 = 12$, $3 + 13 = 16$, $13 + 19 = 32$, $5 + 13 = 18$, $17 + 47 = 64$, and many, many more. However, the statement is *not* true, as one counterexample can show: $2 + 3 = 5$. No number of specific examples will prove that a claim applies to an infinite set, and only one counterexample is necessary to *disprove* a claim.

Reasoning based on a visual representation or story context. With prompting by the teacher and in response to Joshua's skepticism, Mannie and Audrey offer arguments based on representations of addition. Mannie's argument uses a story context and represents addition by combining two classrooms. Audrey combines stacks of cubes to represent addition. Mannie's story and Audrey's manipulation of cubes are both proofs of the general claim that if you add two odd numbers, the sum is an even number. Mannie and Audrey have each developed a mathematical argument. A mathematical proof or argument provides insight into the mathematical relationships that underlie the generalization; it reveals the logic of *why* the claim must be true. Representations are the tools elementary students commonly use to develop arguments. In this book, we call this *representation-based proof.*

The fourth approach listed earlier, making arguments based on the laws of arithmetic, is frequently the focus of formal algebra courses. The "laws of arithmetic" are axioms (basic propositions that are taken to be true) that are the starting point for justifying all the calculations and general claims of arithmetic. These laws include the commutative and associative laws of addition and multiplication and the distributive law of multiplication over addition. Proofs based on these laws are used to justify new general claims that, once proved, can themselves be used in further proofs. But

[Handwritten margin note: Conjecture: statement that is believed to be true but not yet proved.]

this approach to proof is not a beginning point for younger students. In fact, part of the work of the elementary grades is to uncover these laws and to help students see how they characterize the ways the operations work. (See Chapter 9 for more on these laws.)

Mathematical proofs are important because they provide insights into the mathematical relationships that underlie generalizations. By engaging in proof, students learn not just that claims *are* true, but *why* they are true. Because the types of proofs that elementary-aged students can construct are representation-based, the focus of the rest of this chapter will be on this approach.

REPRESENTATION-BASED PROOF

Noticing, articulating, and proving general claims are central to the discipline of mathematics. In the classroom episodes in this section, teachers are supporting students to go beyond solving individual problems to make arguments about an operation for an entire class of numbers. Creating representation-based proofs engages students in forming mental images that capture how the operations work. In doing so, they develop the expectation that mathematics makes sense and deepen their understanding of the meaning and properties of the operations. This operation sense contributes to computational fluency and supports students in making connections between arithmetic and algebra.

A representation-based proof begins with the choice of a way to represent the operation. Examples of representations include number lines, drawings, story contexts, and physical models. The complete representation-based proof includes the picture or model itself, as well as whatever actions students perform using the model and the explanations they offer to demonstrate the truth of the claim. In other words, a complete representation-based proof may include not only a finished picture or physical model but also dynamic elements, such as motions with the model that students either show directly or explain in words.

Consider Mannie's and Audrey's proofs that the sum of two odd numbers is even, from the discussion on page 54. Both arguments include three important attributes:

1. *The meaning of the operation of addition is represented.* Mannie represents addition as combining the students in two classes. Audrey shows addition as joining the stacks of cubes.

2. *The argument does not depend on specific numbers.* Mannie represents an odd number as a class in which all students have partners except one; it doesn't matter how many students are in each class as long as each student has a partner except one. Similarly, Audrey has represented odd numbers as groups of cubes in which every cube but one is paired up, and again, this works for any odd number.

3. _The arguments explain how the conclusion of the claim—that the sum is even—follows from the structure of the representation._ In Mannie's argument, when the students in the two odd-numbered classes are combined, the students without a partner now pair up, so each student has one partner. Thus the number of students in the two classes combined is even. In Audrey's argument, when the two stacks of an odd number of cubes are joined, the unpaired cubes become a pair. Because all cubes are paired, there must be an even number of cubes.

These attributes illustrate general principles for creating complete representation-based proofs. Students must be able to explain how their representations can be interpreted to meet the following criteria:

1. The meaning of the operation(s) involved in the claim is represented with diagrams, manipulatives, or story contexts.

2. The representation can accommodate a class of instances (for example, all whole numbers).

3. The conclusion of the claim follows from the structure of the representation; that is, the representation shows _why_ the statement must be true.

CLASSROOM EXAMPLES OF REPRESENTATION-BASED PROOF

The following examples illustrate students justifying general claims. As you read, consider each general claim for yourself, examine how each operation is represented, experiment with some numerical examples of the claim to get a sense of how the representation applies to a range of examples, and consider how the students use the representation to prove their claim. Each example is followed by a discussion of how well students' justifications match the criteria for representation-based proof.

Example 1: Using a Number Line

Olivia Miller has given her third-grade class the following problem, with the instruction that they should answer the question without carrying out the calculations.

> _Oscar had 90 stickers and decided to share some with his friends. He gave 40 stickers away. Becky also had 90 stickers. She gave away 35 stickers. Who has more stickers now?_

> _Oscar's stickers   90 − 40_

> _Becky's stickers   90 − 35_

Some students have declared that Becky is left with more stickers, claiming, "If you take away a smaller number, you get a bigger number." Now they are working individually or in pairs to investigate this conjecture.

Ms. Miller notices that Kiara is drawing number lines and sits down to discuss Kiara's thinking.

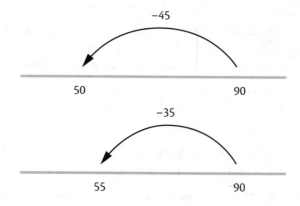

Kiara: I made these because I think it helps me understand what is going on. I can show the subtraction problems on two different number lines. You can see how big my jumps back are.

Ms. Miller: So, how does our generalization, "if you take away a smaller number, you get a bigger number," connect to the number line?

Kiara: Well, see the first one jumps back 40 and lands on 50. The second one jumps back 35 and lands on 55. You can see that the top one has a bigger jump. The 55 is more and that jump is smaller. You start at the same place, but one has a bigger jump and one has a smaller jump.

Ms. Miller: Is there anything else we need to say to clarify our generalization?

Kiara: I think that you have to say that the two problems start with the same number. That was something we said was the same about them. Oh yeah, "smaller number" and "bigger number" could maybe be something like "smaller amount" and "bigger answer."

Ms. Miller: Do you think your strategy of using a number line will work for other sets of related problems like these?

Kiara: It doesn't matter what numbers I put on the number line. It's just going to show that if we start subtracting with the same number, the bigger jump back I go, the smaller the number I land on.

Kiara's picture satisfies the first criterion for representation-based proof by representing subtraction as a jump to the left on the number line. Although her representation matches the specific numbers in the problems, her language indicates that Kiara is thinking more generally about the claim: "It doesn't matter what numbers I put on the number line." That is, her representation can also accommodate subtraction with a class of numbers, satisfying criterion 2.

Kiara goes on to say, "It's just going to show that if we start subtracting with the same number, the bigger jump back I go, the smaller the number I land on." Kiara's conclusion follows from the structure of the number line representation: starting at any point on the number line, the longer the jump to the left (the larger the number that is subtracted), the smaller the value of the point at the end of the jump—that is, the smaller the answer—precisely because it is farther to the left.

As in most of the examples in this book, when Kiara talks about how her representation applies to other numbers, she is thinking of the kinds of numbers she knows about now; for most third graders, these are whole numbers. In later grades, these students might revisit their generalizations to see if they can be extended to other kinds of numbers, for example, to fractions or integers. Particularly as they work with integers, students will need to rethink how subtraction is represented.

Example 2: Using Objects

In Isabel Hazelton's second-grade class, after a student presents the equation, $100 - 87 = 13$, the class is asked to make sure it is correct. Most students check the subtraction by starting at 100 on the hundred chart and counting back 87. If they land on 13, they know the answer is correct. But 87 is a large number to count back, and students understand that it is easy to miscount. Is there another way to check?

Gage suggests starting at 100 and counting back 13 to see if they land at 87. Gage recognizes that if $100 - 13 = 87$, then it must be true that $100 - 87 = 13$. However, his classmates are not convinced.

Ms. Hazelton feels this idea is worth exploring. The next day, she presents the class with $50 - 43 = 7$ and asks them to think about whether this equation is correct. As she checks on individual students, she notices that Gage has written $50 - 7 = 43$. In response to Ms. Hazelton's questions, he shows how he can start at 50 and count back 43 to land on 7, or start at 50 and count back 7 to land on 43.

Gage says, "It works with any subtraction problem. You can switch those two numbers." As the rest of the class continues to work with the original problem, Ms. Hazelton challenges Gage to come up with a way to demonstrate the relationship he sees to the rest of the class.

When whole-class discussion resumes, Gage is prepared with a different representation. He has separated a set of 50 cubes into groups of 43 and 7.

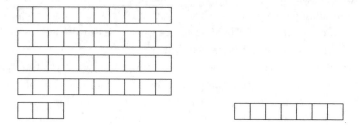

Gage first removes the group of 43, leaving 7, to demonstrate $50 - 43 = 7$. He then replaces the group of 43 and removes the group of 7, leaving 43; $50 - 7 = 43$. He explains that it doesn't matter what numbers you start with. For any subtraction problem, if you subtract one part, you're left with the other.

Gage's argument satisfies the criteria for representation-based proof. Subtraction is represented as removing one part, leaving the other (criterion 1). Any subtraction equation with whole numbers can be represented by a set of cubes separated into two parts (criterion 2). If the first part is removed, the second remains. If the second part is removed, the first remains. Thus, in any subtraction equation, the two parts can be exchanged and the equation remains true (criterion 3).

Although Gage has presented a proof, Ms. Hazelton recognizes that even with the model before them, many of Gage's classmates will need more time and experience to make sense of his argument. To continue the class' thinking, Ms. Hazelton next asks her students to devise story problems that match the equations and could be represented using Gage's arrangement of cubes.

Example 3: Using a Story Context

Like a drawing or physical model, a contextual situation can also embody the actions of an operation on an infinite class of numbers. We revisit the example from Ms. Kaye's third-grade class from Chapter 4 to focus on the use of a story context as the basis for a representation-based proof.

The class has generated a sequence of subtraction expressions that equal 25, and students noticed that both numbers increase by 1:

$$26 - 1$$

$$27 - 2$$

$$28 - 3$$

$$29 - 4$$

As they begin to talk about what this reveals about subtraction, Ms. Kaye suggests that they consider the story context Todd had proposed earlier in the discussion.

> If Todd had 26 baseball cards, and his little brother stole 1, he'd have 25 cards left. What are other numbers of baseball cards Todd could start with and how many would his little brother have to steal so that he would always have 25 cards left?

....

Jonah: If he starts with more, his brother has to take more to get to 25, because there's more cards to take.

Manuel: It's just like . . . he has a bigger number here. So he has to take away more in order to get to the number he wants to get.

Addison: The reason why they're both going up is, since it's higher, then you have to subtract more to get to that, but if it's less, you don't need as much to get to that number. It's less numbers to get to it.

....

In Todd's story context, the meaning of subtraction is represented as removing some number of baseball cards, thus satisfying the first criterion. Although the discussion starts with a specific set of examples, the students' evolving language suggests that their mental images have moved away from the specific numbers—that the representation can accommodate a class of numbers: "It's just like . . . he has a *bigger number* here. So he has to take away *more* in order to get to *the number* he wants to get." Manuel and Addison make an argument that applies to any subtraction expression, and so satisfies the second criterion.

Finally, the conclusion of the claim, that the difference is maintained when both numbers are increased by the same amount, follows from the structure of the story context. Each time more baseball cards are added to Todd's pile, increasing the initial amount, his brother has to remove that many more cards in order for the number of Todd's cards to remain the same. The third criterion is also met.

In all three examples, the representations—whether a number line, cubes, or a story context—are vehicles through which students can show how one situation can be transformed into another and what effect that transformation has on the result: Is equality maintained from the beginning state of the representation to the ending state or not? The representation, the actions performed on or with the representation, and the students' explanations are all needed to create a complete representation-based proof.

HELPING STUDENTS DEVELOP REPRESENTATION-BASED PROOF

How do students learn to reason using representations? What does such reasoning look like at different grade levels? What can a teacher do to help students begin to develop this kind of thinking? The next examples illustrate how teachers craft experiences that orient students to the idea of creating and expanding mathematical arguments.

Creating Arguments for a Specific Instance

Learning that proving is an essential part of mathematics can start early when teachers focus on particular examples of expressions or equations. In the next episode, Ruth Callendar's first-grade students are examining ways to make 10, building a sense of what the operation of addition involves, and becoming familiar with the idea of equivalence. This is familiar work central to first grade. However, the students are also beginning to work on the idea of proof by explaining how they know the expressions are equivalent.

The students have been considering examples of the claim, "Given two addends, if 1 is subtracted from one addend and 1 is added to the other, the sum remains the same" (although they have not stated the idea using this kind of succinct language). One student, Cory, has generated a list of ways to make 10: $5 + 5$, $4 + 6$, $3 + 7$, $2 + 8$, $1 + 9$, and $0 + 10$. Ms. Callendar judges that enough students are confident that these expressions are equivalent for her to ask students to think about *why* this is true.

....

Ms. Callendar: So how did you use this first one, 5 plus 5, to help you with the next one?

Cory: Because if you start out with 5 plus 5, then you . . . and then take 1 away from this 5 and add it to this 6, and then this is 4 and so on and so on.

Ms. Callendar: Can you show me that with these cubes? I am going to give you 5 red cubes and 5 blue cubes for 5 plus 5. Can you show me what you mean, Cory?

Cory: This is what I mean. I mean, so you pretend you have 5 and 5 cubes *[holding up a stack of 5 red cubes and a stack of 5 blue cubes]*. Then put this 5 onto this *[moving 1 blue cube to the red stack]* and that makes this 6 and this 4 and so on and so on until you get to this *[motioning putting the two stacks together to make 10, implying 10 plus 0]*.

Ms. Callendar: Does someone else want to try changing his 4 plus 6 into something else, into the next one? Alice, will you change his 4 plus 6? What are you going to change this 4 plus 6 into, Alice?

Alice: 3 plus 7.

Ms. Callendar *[handing the stacks of cubes to Alice]***: So show us how you are going to do that.**

· ·

Alice moves another blue cube onto the red stack, making a stack of 3 and a stack of 7. The stacks are passed from child to child, and each child changes the stacks, first to 2 and 8, then to 1 and 9, and finally to one stack of 10. Throughout the demonstration, the students are attentive and involved.

The students model the action of addition by joining stacks of cubes. Beginning with a model for 5 + 5, they move the cubes around to produce the other equivalent combinations. Though the students have not yet articulated their argument in words, they have demonstrated why Cory's expressions are all equivalent to 10. These first graders have begun to learn to make mathematical arguments.

Ms. Callendar's role in focusing her students on thinking about a mathematical claim is significant. First, she chooses a sum that is simple for her students to calculate. She draws attention to the relationship between successive expressions in the sequence by asking, "How did you use this first one, 5 plus 5, to help you with the next one?" Then, she suggests students use cubes as a tool to act out what is happening with the numbers. As a result, the students investigate the numerical relationships between expressions while simultaneously deepening their ability to use cubes as a representational tool for their thinking. Ms. Callendar will continue to work with them on using representations to model their ideas and on beginning to put their arguments into words.

Extending an Explanation from One Instance to Additional Instances

Once students have had experience comparing and reasoning about specific pairs of expressions, they are ready for questions that require them to consider how to expand their arguments to include more cases. Olivia Miller's third graders have regularly worked with the "Is the Number Sentence True?" routine. They have focused on pairs of addition expressions, such as $24 + 26 = 25 + 25$, in which one addend is increased by 1 and the other addend is decreased by 1. Now Ms. Miller poses a problem in which the addends are changed by 2.

· ·

Ms. Miller: Yesterday we looked at 24 plus 26 equals 25 plus 25 and decided the number sentence was true. We said it was, without computing. Ana said that we could add 1 to 24 and take that 1 away from 26 to get 25 plus 25. We just changed the problem by ones. I want you to think about another problem now. Is 15 plus 12 equal to 17 plus 10? What do you think?

Is the Number Sentence True?

$$15 + 12 = 17 + 10$$

Ms. Miller [*after a pause, pointing to where they had recorded what Ana had done with the previous example*]: **Could we use this rule? Can you look at the whole problem and think about the strategy that Ana shared with us the other day about "changing the numbers"?**

Jasmine: Ohhh. Just plus 2. Plus 2 to the 15, that's 17, and then 12 take away 2 equals 10.

Ms. Miller: What is Jasmine changing here?

David: She's saying that if we take 2 from 12 and give it to the 15, that makes the 17 that's on the other side. That 12 is now the 10 that's on the other side.

Ms. Miller: I'm noticing something with our two examples. For the first example, we added 1 and took 1 away to make what was on the other side of the equal sign. On the second example, we added 2 and took 2 away. Why is that?

> *Stephanie demonstrates with cubes. She builds the numbers 15 and 12 with a stick of 10 connecting cubes plus the ones needed for each number. Then she takes 2 of the single cubes from the 12 and adds them to the 15. She has transformed 15 + 12 into 17 + 10.*

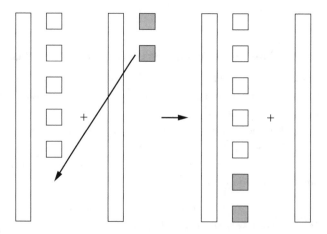

Ms. Miller: Why is this change OK?

···

As with the first-grade class, the third graders are working on ideas about the nature of addition and the meaning of equivalence and are also beginning to work on what it means to prove something in mathematics. Like the first-grade class, the third-grade students build a model with cubes to show how to transform one pair of addends into another. As they engage with specific numbers, they also build awareness that these are examples of a larger class of problems. By offering an example in which 2 is subtracted from one addend and added to the other, Ms. Miller spurs the class to modify their generalization. Stephanie's cube model is a first step toward building a more general argument about adding and subtracting any amount.

IN CONCLUSION . . .

Representation is central to all the work described in this chapter. As students move from single to multiple instances of an idea, the same representations they use to model individual numbers become images useful for representing entire classes of numbers. They are then able to justify their claims based on these representations.

Teachers must explicitly encourage students to use representations to clarify and extend their thinking. As a student creates and describes a representation, that student's thinking becomes visible so that others in the class can comment on it, describe it, raise questions, and compare it with their own images. Teachers often begin by asking students to represent a particular instance of a general claim. After representing and describing one example, students naturally move toward imagining how that image can represent many examples. Their arguments evolve from referencing specific numbers to describing a general class of numbers—"some number," "an amount," and so forth.

The ability to construct arguments about general claims develops continuously over years of mathematical study. To learn about mathematical justification, students must work regularly with many examples and representations over an extended period of time. Each encounter with this work might be a brief ten- to fifteen-minute routine, but through such regular encounters, students develop the habit of thinking about mathematical claims. As students articulate claims, develop mathematical arguments, and modify and expand those arguments, they also strengthen their foundation for understanding the operations and for the development of computational fluency.

In the next chapter, we will examine how students with a range of learning needs work with generalizations and representations. Chapter 7 will then provide groundwork for thinking about students' uses of notation. We will return to the topic of proof in Chapter 8, which includes multiplication and division examples, a focus on how students think through to what numbers their claims apply, and a look at how some students incorporate symbolic notation into their work. As you read on, think about how different students are generalizing: are they just beginning to notice consistencies across problems, articulating a general claim, applying a stated or unstated generalization, or creating a representation-based proof? ∎

FOCUS QUESTIONS

DEVELOPING MATHEMATICAL ARGUMENTS: REPRESENTATION-BASED PROOF

1. The first section of Chapter 5 describes four approaches to justifying a general claim.

    • Reflect on your past work as a math learner. Which of these approaches did you experience?

    • Which approaches are new for you to consider?

    • What are the implications for your own instruction?

2. Chapter 5 continues with a description of the term, *representation-based proof*. For each classroom example (Ms. Miller, Ms. Hazelton, and Ms. Kaye), describe how the students' arguments fit the three criteria. Note any questions that come up for you about interpreting these criteria.

3. Revisit each of the three class episodes (Ms. Miller, Ms. Hazelton, and Ms. Kaye) to identify teacher moves (either questions the teacher asks or math tasks the teacher poses) that push the students to examine the mathematical ideas more deeply. Consider at least one teacher move for each episode: What do you think the teacher's purpose is? What is the impact on the students?

4. In the final two classroom episodes (Ms. Callendar and Ms. Miller), we see students who are working with specific examples rather than general claims. For each classroom episode, explain the mathematical thinking of the students and consider how their thinking is connected to the ideas of representation-based proof.

5. Consider the comments in the conclusion of Chapter 5 and reflect on the math content of your classroom. What are the implications and opportunities for developing this kind of reasoning for the grade level you teach?

6

Focus on the Range of Learners
When Students Struggle and When They Excel

So far you have read about classrooms that include students with a wide range of achievement and confidence in mathematics. Chapter 3 presented descriptions of individual students in two classrooms so you could consider how a range of learners can participate in discussions of general claims about the operations. In this chapter, we again focus on individual students who have been identified by their teachers as either "struggling" or "excelling" in grade-level computation and how instruction that emphasizes the generalizations underlying the behavior of the operations can support them.

Each student described in this chapter has a unique mixture of strengths and needs in mathematics. There are ways in which "excelling" students struggle and "struggling" students excel. You will meet some students who have difficulty with routine grade-level computation and have lost confidence in their ability to do mathematics. Many of these students are receiving extra support. Others described in this chapter have no difficulty with routine grade-level computation, have confidence in their ability, and often need to be challenged to think more deeply.

STUDENTS HAVING DIFFICULTY WITH GRADE-LEVEL COMPUTATION

The development of computational fluency is a major focus in the elementary grades. Students having difficulty with computation often feel they are floundering in mathematics. Even for students strong in other aspects of mathematics, difficulties in computation become a major obstacle to success and confidence in mathematics.

At all grades, students who struggle with computation tend to see each individual problem as a separate endeavor. Although these students may have some knowledge about the behavior of the operations they use, they often attempt to remember the right steps to follow rather than building on what they know about the operations. Their lack of confidence compounds their difficulty and blocks them from using the tools and knowledge they *do* have that might help them.

Another issue for struggling students is continued reliance on counting as a means of computation. In the early grades, counting is an important focus. Young students learn to connect counting words to quantities and to the numerals representing those words and quantities. As they count, students come to see that the quantity represented by each successive numeral in the counting sequence is one more than the quantity represented by the previous numeral. They learn about the oral patterns in the counting sequence and how these patterns connect to the place value structure of the base ten number system. Eventually, they learn to start counting at numbers other than 1 and to count by twos, fives, tens, and other amounts.

Counting is the foundation of the operations. At first, most students use counting by ones to solve addition, subtraction, multiplication, or division problems. However, as students learn more about each operation and its behavior, they should also learn computation strategies deriving from the operation's properties and the structure of the base ten system. It is appropriate for a first grader to solve a subtraction problem by counting backward by ones, but by third grade, that student should have developed more efficient subtraction strategies.

Strong knowledge of the foundations of the operations is critical. Focusing on the actions, representations, and general properties of the operations can help break the cycle in which students move from one individual problem to another without making connections among the problems, rely on counting to be sure of their solution, and do not access what they already know. Instruction that incorporates a focus on general claims links many individual problems and emphasizes the structure and properties of the operation. By explicitly considering general claims, students articulate and understand ideas they can draw on when they face a new computation problem.

We now turn to specific examples in which teachers are working with students to help them:

1. Make connections among problems through reasoning about the operations

2. Make sense of general claims as more than "rules"

3. Make explicit connections between general claims and computation

Making Connections Among Problems Through Reasoning About the Operations

Lydia Rogers provides extra support for students having difficulty with mathematics. Karly is a fourth-grade student in a class Ms. Rogers describes as "comprised of many confident and outspoken" students. Karly presents a mixture of strengths and needs, according to Ms. Rogers:

> *Karly often positions herself at the fringes of our discussions, her concentration shifting as distractions present themselves. Karly struggles to express her ideas verbally, hampered by a borderline communication impairment that does not qualify her for special education support. What Karly lacks in oral expression, she more than makes up for in her ability to create representations of her ideas. Often these representations are basic, yet at times there is an elegance to the simplicity of them.*

Early in the school year, Karly solved the following problem as part of an assessment for a unit on multiplication and division.

√ **7D.** Rosa has 36 erasers that she wants to put in bags, too. She puts the same number of erasers in each bag. How many bags could she pack?

To solve the problem, Karly made many drawings like the one above, using many pages of paper. She put the circles, representing erasers, into groups of many different sizes before settling on the solution above: 4 groups with 9 erasers in each group. When Ms. Rogers asked Karly to explain her solution, this conversation took place:

....

Karly: When I read it, I didn't know anything about how many bags or how many erasers.

Ms. Rogers: Are you saying they didn't give you enough information?

Karly: They didn't say anything about. . . . Well, they say she put the same number of erasers in each bag, but I don't know how much that is, so I just tried to figure it out on tons of papers.

Ms. Rogers [*looking at Karly's pages with different arrangements of circles*]: **So all of theses pages are ways that you tried to arrange 36 erasers into bags? Why did you choose the one that you chose?**

Karly: Because I knew that 10 in 4 bags does not equal 36. It's too much, so I went back a number to 9 and that was my answer. Then I started at 6 and 7 and 8 and 9 and I thought it didn't work and then I went and checked it and it was the one.

Ms. Rogers: When you say that 9 was "the one," what do you mean?

Karly: 9 was the erasers in each bag and I knew there would be 4 bags. I did all those on pieces of paper. I knew that no way it wasn't 9 so I went back and picked it.

···

Before you read on, look back over this interaction. What does Karly understand? What does she need to work on?

Karly understands that solving the problem requires splitting up a quantity into equal groups, and she represents this with drawings. She also makes some sensible decisions about how to proceed when a particular solution does not work; she says, "10 in 4 bags does not equal 36," and understands that if 4 bags with 10 erasers in each bag is more than 36 erasers, one strategy is to try a smaller number of erasers in each bag. However, although she can sometimes conclude that either more or fewer erasers must be in each group, she does not appear to reason from other quantitative information.

Karly's use of trial and error exemplifies how students who struggle with computation tend to treat each arithmetic expression as new and separate, unconnected to any other. Karly made separate attempts to divide the erasers into groups of 10, 9, 8, 7, and 6. Seeing the connections between her trials might have led her to find multiple solutions, as other members of the class were able to do, but Karly was satisfied with one solution. She may have assumed the problem required only one solution, or she may have felt she had done all she could with the problem.

Karly's solution also exemplifies students' overreliance on counting. Her representations appear to rely on counting by ones. She does not call on other knowledge about numbers or operations. For example, Karly does not notice that 36 is an even number, implying one solution of 2 equal groups and another of groups of 2. She tried groups of 6, and it's unclear why she did not notice that 6 groups of 6 is a solution. She may have made a simple counting error; overreliance on counting frequently leads to incorrect solutions due to miscounting.

In January, as Karly's class neared the end of a second unit on multiplication and division, Ms. Rogers met with her to assess her math experience so far that year. In the interim, Ms. Rogers had been working with Karly on the behavior of the operations. She asked Karly to look back at her work on the erasers problem.

....

Ms. Rogers: How many answers do you think there are to this problem?

Karly: Tons of them.

Ms. Rogers: So you *do* think there is more than one answer?

Karly: You can split them up. Well, no, you can't split a 9 up. Oh, you could do it in threes. You would go to . . . 12 bags.

Ms. Rogers: So if you had 3 in each bag, you'd need how many bags?

Karly: I don't know. . . . 1 bag *[of 9]* equals 3 bags of 3 and there are 4 of them, so I know 3 plus 3 equals 6 and there's another 2 *[threes]* so it's 6 plus 6 so it equals 12. 6 plus 6 plus 6 plus 6 equals 12—no—3 plus 3 plus 3 plus 3 equals 12.

Ms. Rogers: Do you have that possibility on any of your sheets?

Karly: I don't know what I did. I did 8 plus 8 plus 8 plus 8. It was under 36. It was 2 less. . . . There are two answers for that problem. 9 times 4 and you can spread them out into threes. It's 3 in each bag so it's 3 times 12 equals 36. And then there's 12 bags with 3 in them.

Ms. Rogers: So what does the 12 mean?

Karly: It's 12 bags.

....

The associative property of multiplication underlies Karly's idea about splitting up bags. Karly first visualizes splitting the erasers into 4 bags of 9 erasers. She then divides each bag into 3 new bags. That is, each group of 9 erasers can be split up into 3 groups, each containing 3 erasers. We could represent her idea, so far, like this: $4 \times 9 = 4 \times (3 \times 3)$.

Karly appears to be making the following argument: When I split each 9 into 3 threes, each of my original 4 groups now has 3 smaller groups. I now have $3 + 3 + 3 + 3$ groups, or 12 groups. We can extend the notation above to represent her reasoning: $4 \times 9 = 4 \times (3 \times 3) = (4 \times 3) \times 3 = 12 \times 3$. The equation, $4 \times (3 \times 3) = (4 \times 3) \times 3$, is an example of the associative property of multiplication. This property is expressed more generally as: $a \times (b \times c) = (a \times b) \times c$.

The story context helps Karly keep track of the number of bags and the number of erasers per bag. One interesting aspect of this episode is how quickly Karly "sees" both the new amount in the bags and the new number of bags: "Oh, you could do it in threes. You would go to . . . 12 bags." Once the teacher questions her, she gives a more complete explanation of her thinking, though she initially responded as if she had seen the new arrangement all at once. The story context provides an image of division as "splitting," which makes sense to her as a way to generate a new arrangement of groups of erasers.

It is clear that Karly often lacks confidence in her own math thinking and ideas. She is quick to answer "I don't know" to a question, even when it turns out that she does know. She is not strong at computing, even with fairly easy numbers. (She incorrectly states that $8 + 8 + 8 + 8$ is 2 less than 36.) She still does not see that there are even more possibilities for dividing 36 into equal groups. She either does not know all of her multiplication facts or is not accessing them to help her with this problem.

To help Karly learn to make general claims about multiplication, Ms. Rogers will work with her in a way that enables her to make connections among problems, become clearer about the behavior of the operations, and then apply what she knows about the operations to solve problems. For example, Karly's use of a story context to reason about multiplication indicates a strength the teacher can build upon. By using drawings to represent this story and others, Karly can begin to make connections among different multiplication expressions. Ms. Rogers writes, "My goals for Karly include providing frequent opportunities for her to use her representations as links to bigger ideas and then to connect these ideas and representations to their more symbolic notation in equations."

Making Sense of General Claims as More Than "Rules"

Students who are having difficulty with a problem sometimes grasp at rules and procedural steps that they think they can rely on. Sometimes they remember and apply these rules correctly, and sometimes they do not. When students have not investigated these rules by using representations or story contexts to ground the rules in images, they may be able to apply the rules mechanically in some situations, but not recognize how to apply them in others.

For example, at another point in Karly's interview, Ms. Rogers asks her whether she can change the order of two factors to solve a problem—for example, to think of 12×3 as 3×12. Karly knows that these two expressions result in the same product and explains in a procedural way: "You put the 12 where the 3 is and the 3 where the 12 is." However, when asked in the context of the story problem, "Is there another way to arrange the erasers using the numbers 3 and 12?" Karly is not able to answer. Karly "knows" the rule but does not connect it to her representation of multiplication. She may not even envision the erasers problem as involving multiplication; her approach may rely largely on counting and addition.

Students need to develop images such as representations and story contexts in order to have a working knowledge of the properties and behaviors of operations. Once students have developed strong images of the actions of the operations, they can call on these images to solve problems and to articulate and apply rules with meaning.

The following episode illustrates the work of a fifth grader, Nathan, in multiplication and how he is coming to make sense of a rule that his class has articulated:

In a multiplication expression, doubling one factor and halving another factor doesn't change the product.

Nathan's teacher, Arthur MacAllister, describes him this way:

Nathan is a very pleasant young man who is very interested in sports and pleasing others. Nathan has struggled in mathematics throughout his elementary school years and has developed a strong sense of anxiety toward many math tasks. He has a medical diagnosis for this anxiety and is often discouraged when faced with difficulty. He has no diagnosed learning disabilities, but struggles in a similar way as those who do. Nathan is willing to speak up during classroom conversations, but I am often left wondering how much he truly understands and how much he is merely repeating the words of his classmates and myself. Nathan scored very low on the fourth-grade end-of-grade test and came into my class with very little number sense or mathematical confidence.

Nathan's class has spent a great deal of time focusing on generalizations about multiplication. Early in the year, the class was considering the equation $2 \times 12 = 4 \times 6$. Mr. MacAllister had the following exchange with Nathan and Gannon, who were working together. The boys had built arrays with square tiles.

⋯⋯⋯⋯⋯⋯⋯⋯⋯⋯⋯⋯⋯⋯⋯

Mr. MacAllister: What are you guys looking at there?

Gannon: I built a 2 by 12 and that's 24, and Nathan built a 4 by 6 and that's 24 too.

Mr. MacAllister: Can you show me with the tiles why they're the same? What do you think, Nathan?

Nathan: They're both 24. They just are. They're the same.

⋯⋯⋯⋯⋯⋯⋯⋯⋯⋯⋯⋯⋯⋯⋯

As the class continued working on the idea that doubling one factor while halving the other doesn't change the product, Nathan participated but computed answers to show that two expressions were equivalent rather than reasoning about the relationship between them.

In January, Mr. MacAllister grabs ten minutes alone with Nathan to check his understanding. Nathan is anxious, so Mr. MacAllister presents him with a problem involving very accessible numbers. That way, Nathan can concentrate on general ideas about the operation of multiplication.

$$12 \times 3 = 6 \times \underline{\quad}$$

Nathan: Well, I would think of a story. Like . . . I had 12 cookies in each box and 3 boxes. That's the same as 6 boxes of what size? It's still like a multiplying *and* a division problem.

Mr. MacAllister: Tell me more about that.

Nathan: Well, I would say you would multiply 12 by 3 and then do the same thing here. So it's like 6 times 6. [*At this point, Nathan kind of mutters "12 times 3 is 36 and 6 times 6 is 36," then nods.*] Yeah, it works. It's 6 in the blank.

Mr. MacAllister: Can you draw what is happening here? Like by using dot patterns or something?

Nathan: Okay, so it's 12 times 3, so that's like 12, 3 rows of 12, like the 3 boxes of cookies.

Nathan draws 3 columns of 12 dots and boxes each column.

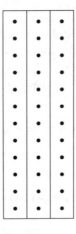

Nathan: But then it's like you have the same number of cookies but you have 6 boxes instead of 3. To have it be 36, it has to be 6 cookies each.

Mr. MacAllister: So, what was the change in the number of cookies in each box?

Nathan: Six . . . it's like half as many. . . .

Mr. MacAllister: Can you show that in your drawing?

Nathan draws a horizontal line, cutting the 3 columns in half.

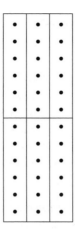

Mr. MacAllister: So, what did that do to the number of groups?

Nathan: It went up by 3. . . . It doubled. . . . It's like what we did in class those times, the doubling and halving thing.

Mr. MacAllister uses the interview to make sure Nathan is not simply parroting what he has heard often in class. By working with manageable numbers, Nathan is able to relax and ground his thinking in images, first the story about cookies in a box and then a diagram to represent that story. He is able to explain that when the number of boxes is doubled, the number of cookies in each box is cut in half. He also has a sense of the operations he is using: "It's . . . like a multiplying *and* a division problem." He may be thinking that the number of boxes has been multiplied by 2 and the number of cookies per box has been divided in half, or that he multiplies 12 × 3 to get a total of 36 cookies, then divides that 36 by 6 to get the new number of cookies per box. There are glimpses of both of these ideas in what he says and what he shows in his diagram.

Nathan still does not articulate a general claim, but he does see what he has done as an example of "the doubling and halving thing." The work on generalization has supported Nathan to develop images of multiplication with which he can reason. The focus on connections among multiplication problems helps strengthen his understanding of the behavior of the operations. With this understanding, Nathan is less likely to simply grab at poorly remembered rules and procedures when solving an unfamiliar problem.

Making Explicit Connections Between General Claims and Computation

Once representations and arguments for the behavior of an operation have been developed, they can be applied to computation problems. In the example that follows, Lorraine Vasquez helps fourth-grader Alondra make an explicit connection between a behavior of an operation and its use in computation. Ms. Vasquez provides extra support outside the regular classroom to students who are having difficulty in mathematics. Alondra came to Ms. Vasquez unable to solve two- and three-digit addition problems. Ms. Vasquez hopes that building Alondra's understanding of the operation of addition will help Alondra develop strategies to solve addition problems. Ms. Vasquez describes Alondra as follows:

> *Alondra repeated third grade. Yet her math understanding and thinking did not benefit from staying one more year in grade 3. Alondra doesn't have confidence in her capacity to do math. She is still struggling with simple computations, relies on her fingers, and counts on by ones for addition and back by ones for subtraction. She has no knowledge of combinations of ten, doubles, or doubles plus/minus one. She has trouble remembering the number sequence in the hundreds and is very attached to the traditional algorithm, even for solving, for example, 100 + 80. Alondra has never attempted to decompose numbers to operate when left on her own.[1]*

Alondra's reliance on counting and learned procedural steps, both of which she applies indiscriminately, holds her back from using reliable computation methods with confidence.

Ms. Vasquez has been working with Alondra's group on equivalent addition expressions. In December, Alondra is not able to reason about equations such as 59 + 26 = 49 + 36. With help, she might model the problem with cubes to show that both expressions are equal to 85, but she cannot reason about why the sums must be equal without computing. Over the next two months, Ms. Vasquez emphasizes the use of story contexts to help students model equivalent addition expressions. First, she offers her own story context to the students, and then challenges students to come up with their own. In February, the group is working together to create a problem equivalent to 395 + 268 that is easier to solve:

---

1   The phrase "count on by ones" refers to starting with one addend, then counting up to add a second addend. For example, to add 9 + 5, the student starts at 9, then counts 10, 11, 12, 13, 14, keeping track in some way (sometimes by using fingers) that exactly 5 more numbers are counted in the counting sequence. Counting back by ones for subtraction involves a similar double count—for example, for 12 − 4, the student counts 11, 10, 9, 8, keeping track of counting back 4 times, with the final number (8) representing the difference. "Combinations of ten, doubles, and doubles plus/minus one" are common classifications for addition facts. *Combinations of ten* include facts such as 6 + 4 and 7 + 3; the set of *doubles* includes facts such as 6 + 6 and 7 + 7; and the set of *doubles plus/minus one* includes facts such as 5 + 6 and 8 + 7, which students typically solve by relating them to doubles.

Ms. Vasquez: Can 400 plus 263 help us solve the initial problem? Can you think about it without solving the problem? Try to look at the numbers carefully before you answer.

Malik: Yes, that problem is easier.

Ms. Vasquez: Can that problem help us solve 395 plus 268?

Alondra: Yeah!, we are taking . . . we are taking, hold on . . . well, we are taking something from 268 and putting it in 395.

Ms. Vasquez: So how much are you taking?

Malik: 5! To get to 400 from 395 is 5 more!

Alondra [after counting on her fingers]**:** Yes, 5. So you take 5 from 268.

Ms. Vasquez: Would you be able to come up with a story problem that will explain what is happening with these numbers?

Working with Malik, Alondra then comes up with a context to justify her idea. She writes:

There are 395 butterflies in one boxes in the other box there 268 then we put 5 to the 395 box and that becomes 400. 268 box becomes 263.

Over the next few months, Alondra begins solving addition problems by creating equivalent problems that are easier for her to solve. However, she often needs prompting to do so. Ms. Vasquez works on helping Alondra and the rest of the group to access and apply their understanding that parts of addends can be rearranged without changing the sum. In May, when Alondra is asked to find an equivalent expression for 585 + 237 "so that you can solve it in your head," Alondra first generates 605 + 217, then changes that to 600 + 222, which she solves easily. Although still requiring some prompting, Alondra is well on her way to using and applying her knowledge about the behavior of addition.

Students like Alondra, who are so far behind their peers in solving routine problems, need problem-solving tools they understand and can apply. For Alondra, the most important goal is not necessarily to use the quickest computation method but to develop more efficient strategies. These strategies should use tools she can rely on, that make sense to her, and in which she has confidence. The image of boxes of butterflies (and other story contexts the students use in Ms. Vasquez's class) helps Alondra remain confident about subtracting an amount from one addend and adding to the other. By visualizing the butterflies moving from box to box, she understands what she is doing with the numbers and why it works.

The students we have discussed in this section reap benefits from a focus on noticing and using ideas about regularities across problems. The teachers' knowledge of the generalizations that underlie computation guides their instructional choices to engage students who have difficulty thinking about mathematics. Students who have difficulty solving computation problems make the most progress by engaging in true mathematical thinking (not just solving large numbers of problems), weaving connections across many problems, building a solid foundation for learning, and applying methods that make sense and can be generalized.

STUDENTS WHO EXCEL IN GRADE-LEVEL COMPUTATION

Some students easily solve computation problems that their grade-level peers find difficult. These students may be confident in mathematics and eager to participate in math class. They may come to an answer quickly and say they "just knew" the answer. Teachers often wonder how to challenge and engage these students. But students who excel in computation also have a range of strengths and needs. Some students considered "good at math" have a restricted view of what mathematics is and what it means to engage with mathematical ideas. Others do not think of themselves as competent math thinkers, even though their teachers see that they excel at many classroom tasks. Students who find correct answers easily may never have been challenged to think about the characteristics and properties of the operations that underlie the strategies they use to get their answers. When offered this challenge, they may be eager to engage in these new kinds of questions, or they may become frustrated by unfamiliar questions and be unprepared to use errors as a source of learning.

Moving Beyond the Comfort Zone of Correct Answers

A focus on articulating, representing, and justifying general claims supports students to go deeper in their thinking about numbers and operations, starting even in the primary grades. Elizabeth is a first-grade student who has a good grasp of the number sequence, understands how numbers are composed of tens and ones, knows her addition facts, and can mentally add one-digit and some two-digit numbers (for example, multiples of five and ten). In these areas, she is well ahead of her peers, most of whom are working on single-digit addition.

In January, her teacher, Robert Williams, meets with her to look at equivalent addition expressions. They start with one-digit addends, such as $6 + 2 = 7 + 1$. Elizabeth uses cubes to represent the addends:

....

Elizabeth: 6 is lower than 7 and 2 is higher than 1, so I think it balances each other. Both have one higher number and one lower number.

Then, Mr. Williams gives her some equations to solve:

$$9 + 3 = 8 + ?$$

Elizabeth: I can make it a true sentence by replacing the question mark with a 4.

Mr. Williams: Why?

Elizabeth: I know that, I sort of do the 10 trick with the 9, but I know that 9 is 1 less than 10. So, instead of doing 13, I do 12 because I know that 9 is 1 less than 10.

Mr. Williams *[erasing the question mark and writing a 4]*: **Do you see the pattern that you were talking about earlier?**

Elizabeth: Yes, 9 is 1 more higher than 8 and 3 is 1 less than 4.

Mr. Williams: Now I want to work with some bigger numbers. I want you to think about the patterns that we have been talking about. Rather than trying to add the numbers to figure out the answer, try to think about the patterns.

$$39 + 11 = 40 + ?$$

Elizabeth: Put a 10 there.

Mr. Williams: Why?

Elizabeth: I think it works because I saw an 11 and 39 and I knew that 11 is higher than 10 by 1 more and 40 was higher than 39. So I thought it was a 10.

Mr. Williams: Do you know what 40 and 10 is?

Elizabeth: 50.

Mr. Williams: Which number sentence is easier to solve, 39 plus 11 or 40 plus 10?

Elizabeth: 40 plus 10.

As Mr. Williams listens to Elizabeth solve these problems, he wonders what would happen if he presents her with a problem in which one addend is increased by 2 instead of by 1. He gives her the following problem:

$$28 + 16 = 30 + ?$$

Mr. Williams: Share what you are thinking.

Elizabeth: I think it is a 15.

Mr. Williams: Now why do you think it is 15?

Elizabeth: I see 16 so maybe it would be 15.

Mr. Williams: Why do you think so?

Elizabeth: Because 15 is 1 lower than 16. But . . . now I think it is not true because now I saw the 28 and it could be true but if I did, um, I don't think it's right. It could be 14 or 15.

Mr. Williams: You said you were looking at the 28. How did that help you?

Elizabeth: That 28 is 2 lower than 30 so it may be 14.

Mr. Williams: So you think the change in these numbers has to be the same? 28 is 2 less than 30 so this number has to be 2 less than 16?

Elizabeth: Uh-huh.

Mr. Williams: What I am noticing is that you are seeing how the patterns can help you make the numbers easier to work with.

Elizabeth: I already finished my second-grade adding book . . . in kindergarten!

Mr. Williams: I can see that is really helping! Let's do one more.

. . . .

As Elizabeth tackles $39 + 11 = 40 + ?$, she seems to understand that if "both [expressions] have one higher number and one lower number," the sums are equal. But when presented with a problem in which 2 is added to one of the addends, requiring that 2 be subtracted from the other to create an equivalent expression, she does not expand her rule immediately to take into account that the difference between 28 and 30 is 2, not 1. She has to rethink the general rule she was applying and is much less sure of how to create an equivalent expression, as is made clear by her language: "I don't think it's right. It could be 14 or 15." Mr. Williams doesn't take her ease in solving the first few problems at face value; he probes to find the limitations of her ideas in order to decide on the next steps to take with her.

Mr. Williams has found a way to challenge Elizabeth to think more deeply about addition. Just as the math becomes more difficult for her, she states, almost as if defending her status as a "good" math student, "I already finished my second-grade adding book . . . in kindergarten!" Although working on math problems that she cannot solve quickly and easily is frustrating to Elizabeth in the short term, in the long term she has the opportunity to engage with mathematical ideas in a way that challenges and expands her understanding. Goals for Elizabeth and other students who easily master core grade-level content should go beyond getting correct answers to individual problems. They need to enter new territory for which they do not have ready-made tools and procedures and, eventually, learn to pose and investigate their own questions about connections across problems.

Trishna, a third grader in Alice Kaye's class, is another student who needs to move beyond solving individual problems. Ms. Kaye starts every day with a discussion of the factors of the number of days they've been in school (for example, on day 20, they talk about the factors of 20). As the year progresses, students record conjectures about the factors of different numbers and make predictions about the factors of the next number. At the beginning of the year, Trishna's mother told Ms. Kaye that Trishna, who was competent in all her grade-level computation work, was "bored" with these discussions. However, as time went on, Trishna, with Ms. Kaye's support, began to find in these discussions ideas that intrigued her and challenged her to think more deeply about mathematics and to formulate and articulate mathematical arguments.

Here is part of a discussion from December. One of the general claims on the class list is, "You can't count to any odd number by 2." The question comes up, "Can you count to an odd number by *any* even number?" In other words, the students are discussing whether an odd number can ever have an even factor. Trishna participates in this discussion with attention and conviction:

....

Ms. Kaye: Is it possible that we're going to find an odd number that we could break apart into evens?

Most of the class: No!

Ms. Kaye: No? Never? Even though we haven't tried every odd number in the whole world, have we?

Julia: That would take way too long!

Ms. Kaye: So, Julia, I guess that's the point I'm pushing on here right now. How do we know that, even though we haven't tried every single odd number? So, what can we offer as proof of that?

Evan: You haven't built up enough for another 2. You only have 1 more.

Trishna: I'm just saying another reason why I absolutely positively know that if you can't do twos you can't do any even number. . . . It's almost like 2 *is* every single even number, because you can *always* find 2 in every single even number. So, it's like 2 is all the even numbers. But you can't find fours in every single even number.

Ms. Kaye: But, if you had fours . . . If I could break this number today up into fours . . .

Trishna [*emphatically*]**:** You'd also *have* to have twos. 2 is in every single even number.

....

Trishna's claim is based on the idea that if some number, c, is a factor of another number, n, then any factors of c must also be factors of n. For example, 4 is a factor of 20, so 20 can be divided evenly into fours. Because 2 is a factor of 4, those fours can be further divided into twos. The 20, therefore, can also be divided into twos, so 2 is also a factor of 20.

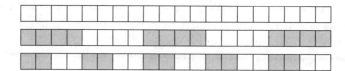

Trishna argues that, because 2 is a factor of any even number, if any even number is a factor of some number, n, 2 must also be a factor of n. Because the class has already agreed that an odd number does not have a factor of 2, she concludes that it cannot have any other even factor.[2]

At the end of the year, Ms. Kaye asks Trishna about her change in attitude toward the class' mathematical discussions. Trishna comments both on what she is getting out of the discussions and how she views these discussions as a collaborative enterprise:

I have never been in a class where we talked about stuff like that before. It's like taking the number and bringing it alive, making it much bigger. 88 is not just like 2 eights next to each other. It's also a count of 11.

We have so many theories, and that's got me thinking. I talk about it at home all the time. This morning, I woke up and told my mom that today was a prime number, and she said, "What?" When we're all thinking about it together, we have 21 ideas. It's not just me thinking about it for myself.

Trishna could almost be Elizabeth, the first grader with whom this section began, two years later and with an expanded view of what it means to engage with and be competent in mathematics.

Taking Time to Look for Connections

Students like Elizabeth and Trishna who solve computation problems easily may tend to solve them automatically without checking whether their solutions make sense. Students who have good intuitions about how to approach a problem may still need help to recognize, articulate, identify, extend, and apply the ideas they are using. By recognizing students' needs to articulate, examine, and generalize the principles that underlie their work, teachers can help students more carefully consider what they are doing and why, and how they can apply their understanding to other situations. The next episode illustrates such an interaction.

We first saw Ben, a second grader in Isabel Hazelton's class, in Episode A of Chapter 3 (p. 25). In a class discussion, Ben had some important ideas to offer, but also showed some confusion that he sorted out by visualizing addition and subtraction on the

---

2 Trishna is using an important kind of mathematical argument—reasoning by contradiction: If mathematical reasoning that starts with the conjecture one is testing (in this case, that an odd number can have an even factor) leads to a statement that contradicts something that has already been proven or defined (in this case, that an odd number would have to have a factor of 2), then the conjecture is false.

number line. Although Ben has strong computation skills in comparison to his peers, he has his own needs. Like Elizabeth, sometimes he is satisfied by just getting the correct answer. His teacher writes:

> *Before we went on winter break, I was encouraging Ben to change one expression in order to generate a new equivalent expression. I've also been reminding him to create models to show his thinking. My sense is that Ben has mental images for his ideas, but he is reluctant to find ways for making his ideas visible to others. He is a strong math thinker. I think it's important to challenge Ben to explore how he can share his ideas.*

One day in January, Ms. Hazelton asks her students to generate expressions equivalent to 18. Ben writes in his math log:

$$2 + 2 + 2 + 2 + 2 + 2 + 2 + 2 + 2$$

$$3 + 3 + 3 + 3 + 3 + 3$$

$$4 + 4 + 4 + 4 + 2$$

$$5 + 5 + 5 + 3$$

$$6 + 6 + 6$$

$$7 + 7 + 4$$

$$8 + 8 + 2$$

$$9 + 9$$

Stop and think about what ideas Ben might be using intuitively. Which ideas could be fruitfully pursued? If you were Ben's teacher, what might you ask him about his list of expressions?

Here is Ben's interaction with Ms. Hazelton:

....

Ben: I was trying to do doubles. I knew that fours will not work because 2 will be left over and fives will not work because 18 is not in the fives.

> *I thought Ben was using the term doubles to mean counting by a given number. English is not Ben's first language and his use of words can be unclear. I wanted to be sure I understood what he was thinking.*

Ms. Hazelton: What do you mean "18 is not in the fives"?

Ben: If you count by fives, it's not a counting by 5 number. I knew sixes will work, because I know 9 plus 9 will work and 6 plus 6 plus 6 will work because if you give 3 to that 6 it will be a 9 and if you give 3 to that 6 it will be a 9, too.

> *Ben was pointing to the third 6 and indicating that he could break it apart into threes. He was explaining how 9 plus 9 can be derived from 6 plus 6 plus 6.*

Ms. Hazelton: So you started with twos and showed that twos will work and threes will work. How did you know that fours wouldn't work?

Ben: I just knew it.

Ms. Hazelton: Were you thinking that you wouldn't have enough twos to make another 4? Or did you just know that 18 isn't a counting by 4 number?

Ben: I just knew 18 wasn't a counting by 4 number because you can count to 8 by fours, but by 10, you can't count by fours. And 10 plus 8 equals 18.

Ms. Hazelton: Oh, so you broke the 18 apart and thought about it as 10 and 8. You knew that 8 would work, but the 10 wouldn't work.

Ben: Yes.

Ms. Hazelton: Interesting. What about 7 plus 7 plus 4? What were you thinking about ahead of time for that one? Do you remember?

Ben: No.

Ms. Hazelton: Did you know that 7 plus 7 equals 14, then you added on 4?

Ben: Yeah, I just added 2 from the sixes.

Ms. Hazelton: You added 2 from the sixes?

Ben: I added 1 from the 6 and put it over there [indicating the first addend in 6 plus 6 plus 6]. Then I added another 1 from the 6 and put it over there.

Ms. Hazelton: You thought about it as breaking apart this 6 and you would have to take 2 to make each of these sixes 1 more to get your sevens.

Ben: I kept on adding 1 to here and another 1 there.

Ms. Hazelton: You took apart the third number so that you could increase the other two numbers?

Ben: Yeah.

Ms. Hazelton: Then did you do the same thing with 8 plus 8 plus 2?

Ben: Yeah.

Ms. Hazelton: Interesting.

....

Ms. Hazelton wrote, "As we finished our conversation, a grin of satisfaction spread over Ben's face. He seemed to be articulating his ideas for himself as we talked."

As Ms. Hazelton examines Ben's list of expressions and talks with him, she recognizes he is thinking systematically about his expressions. She doesn't simply accept

Ben's facility and offer a compliment, but takes this opportunity to stop by his desk and ask him to explain his ideas. Through questioning and restating his ideas, she emphasizes that she is interested in how Ben thinks. She shows that she values his reflection on his work.

The kinds of questions Ms. Hazelton asks force Ben to examine his own thinking. For example, when explaining why 18 cannot be split evenly into fours, Ben begins by saying he "just knew," but then he is able to articulate and clarify his ideas in response to his teacher's questions. By accepting the explanation "I just knew it" from students who solve problems easily, teachers lose a chance to help them become aware of their own mathematical thinking so they can develop tools to solve problems when they don't "just know." Instead, Ms. Hazelton engages Ben with mathematics in a deeper way by challenging him to articulate the principles that underlie his facility with numbers. Judging from his reaction to this brief conversation with his teacher, Ben finds satisfaction in developing and using mathematical reasoning.

Ben is only talking about the number 18, and not explicitly making more general claims. However, at several points he seems to articulate examples of what, for him, are general principles. For example, he explains that one way to determine if 18 is a multiple of 4 is to see if he can split it into two parts, each of which is a multiple of 4. He claims that because one addend (8) is a multiple of 4 but the other addend (10) is not, the sum cannot be a multiple of 4. This conjecture could provide an opening for Ben to represent and justify his ideas in a class discussion, thereby engaging other class members in articulating his general claim and investigating whether it works with other numbers.

IN CONCLUSION . . .

Mathematics instruction that focuses on general claims about the operations benefits both students who struggle with grade-level computation and students who excel at it. Such instruction provides all students with access to the meaning and properties of operations. It builds the foundation of computational fluency and connects arithmetic and algebra. Although these overall goals apply to all students, different students benefit in different ways.

For students having difficulty, a focus on properties of the operations supports computational fluency based on images and principles that connect individual problems. This work also expands students' understanding of the meaning of the operations and their underlying properties. We disadvantage students if we assume that learners who are having difficulty with some aspects of classroom mathematics cannot do this kind of thinking, but can only solve individual problems and focus on specific computation strategies. A focus on generalizations helps students who are having difficulty with grade-level computation problems to:

- make connections among problems based on properties of the operations so that each individual problem is not a separate piece of work;

- rely more on reasoning about the operations and less on counting or on trying to remember rules without understanding them;

- develop and use images of the operations they can call on to solve problems; and

- apply generalizations to support them in solving computation problems.

Students who easily solve grade-level computation problems also benefit from digging more deeply into the mathematics that underlies the operations. The contributions of these students can be catalysts for other students' thinking, while simultaneously helping the contributing student attain a deeper understanding of mathematics. Students for whom routine grade-level mathematics comes easily may still need to learn how to think and reason in mathematics, and they may not have learned how to consider other students' ideas. A focus on generalizing helps these students to:

- articulate underlying properties of the operations so that they can examine and reason about them;

- learn to use their mental images of the operations in order to expand their thinking about general claims; and

- move beyond the comfort zone of correct answers to pose mathematical questions and wonder about mathematical connections.

Maintaining a focus on representing, articulating, and justifying general claims about the operations also helps all students experience the excitement of discovering and understanding important mathematical ideas and learn to pose, investigate, and justify their own mathematical conjectures.

In this and previous chapters, we have stressed the central role of representing the operations. Nathan uses a story about boxes of cookies that he then represents in a diagram; Alondra imagines butterflies in two boxes. Symbolic notation is another kind of representation. In the next chapter, we will see how students use symbolic notation to express their ideas, and we will also examine issues that arise as students begin to use algebraic notation. ■

FOCUS QUESTIONS

FOCUS ON THE RANGE OF LEARNERS: WHEN STUDENTS STRUGGLE AND WHEN THEY EXCEL

1. **The classroom interviews and discussions in Chapter 6 illustrate how math instruction that emphasizes generalizations that underlie the behavior of the operations can support both learners who are having great difficulty with grade-level computation and learners who find grade-level computation to be quite easy for them.**

   • What connections do you see between the students described in this chapter and your own students?

   • What questions about teaching or about learning does this chapter raise?

2. **Consider the student discussion in Chapter 6 from Lydia Rogers' class as an opportunity to analyze student thinking and teacher moves.**

   • Explain Karly's thinking at the beginning, middle, and end of the episode.

   • What is the math idea that Karly is working on?

   • Explain the connections between Karly's drawings and this math idea.

   • Examine the questions Ms. Rogers poses. In what ways does she both support and challenge Karly?

3. **Consider the student discussion in Chapter 6 from Arthur McAllister's class.**

   • Explain Nathan's thinking at the beginning, middle, and end of the interview.

   • What is the math idea that Nathan is working on?

   • Explain the connections between Nathan's drawings and this math idea.

   • Examine the questions Mr. McAllister poses. In what ways does he both support and challenge Nathan?

4. **Consider the student interview with Elizabeth in Chapter 6 from Robert Williams' class.**

   • Explain Elizabeth's thinking at the beginning, middle, and end of the interview.

   • Examine the questions Mr. Williams poses. In what ways does he support and challenge Elizabeth?

5. **Consider the student interview with Ben in Chapter 6 from Isabel Hazelton's class.**

   • Explain Ben's thinking at the beginning, middle, and end of the interview.

   • Examine the questions Ms. Hazelton poses. In what ways does she support and challenge Ben?

7

Learning Algebraic Notation
Looking at Two Things at Once

Algebra provides a concise and powerful notational system. It is used to state and prove generalizations, represent functions, model situations, and solve problems. The introduction of variables—letters that stand for unspecified numbers—is a key innovation of this system of notation.

However, algebraic notation makes sense to students only if each of the symbols carries meaning for them. Understanding of algebraic notation builds on an understanding of the arithmetic symbols: +, −, ×, ÷, and =. In particular, students must develop an understanding of the equal sign consistent with its use in algebra. Deep algebraic understanding cannot be accomplished by students who merely learn to manipulate symbols.

The work of noticing and articulating arithmetic generalizations provides a context to create meaning for notation. Using a variety of representations generates images for students to hold in mind that capture mathematical relationships. By keeping these images in mind while expressing the relationships in algebraic notation, students deepen their understanding of the notation.

This chapter examines the potential and challenges involved in developing meaning for notation. We begin with cases in which students extend their understanding of arithmetic symbols in a way that will support development of fluency with algebraic symbols. Then we consider cases where students express their thinking through algebraic notation.

MAKING MEANING FOR ARITHMETIC SYMBOLS

In the early grades, children work on problems and play games involving combining and separating numbers in a variety of contexts. These activities help them develop an understanding of what addition and subtraction do. Through such activities, students begin to learn the use of symbolic notation. For example, $7 + 3 = 10$ might represent having 7 cubes and receiving 3 additional cubes, for a total of 10 cubes; or the same equation might represent 7 girls and 3 boys, for a total of 10 children.

Once students begin to use the notation, it is important that they continue to associate the symbols with meaning. Manipulatives and story contexts are not merely "crutches" for students who have difficulty but are essential tools for all students to reason about operations and provide meaning for symbols. Consider the following episodes about first and third graders engaged in such work.

Connecting Actions to Equations

A first-grade class has been working on finding pairs of numbers that make 5, 6, 10, and so forth. They have employed a variety of story contexts (red and green apples that fit in a box, children on the upper and lower levels of a bunk bed) and a variety of representations (coloring in squares to show red and green apples, using different colored cubes for the two addends). On this day, they are working on ways to make 8.

The teacher, Rachel Lewis, presents an egg carton with 8 spaces for eggs. Starting with 8 blue eggs in the egg carton, the class replaces blue eggs with white eggs, one by one, with a student recording number sentences on a poster.

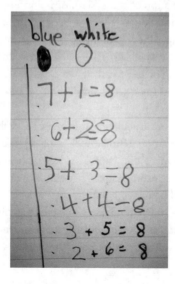

Although the students successfully represent the combinations in symbols, Ms. Lewis recognizes that there is more to learn about the symbols beyond writing number sentences correctly. As the recorder is about to write *1 + 7 = 8* on the poster, Ms. Lewis says, "Everyone just watch Talia as she writes this equation. Raise your hand if you see a pattern in our equations. Let's give everyone thinking time." Several students have ideas.

· ·

Kamala: 7, 6, 5, 4, 3, 2, 1. It's all going down.

David: The pluses are all in a row, and the equals. All of the eights are there. They all equal 8. The carton fills with numbers until it gets to 8.

The students see some patterns in the symbols: The first addend decreases by 1 in each line; the addition sign and the equal sign appear in the same positions in each line; the sum is always equal to 8. Ms. Lewis now asks questions to help the students realize how these patterns connect to the action of replacing blue eggs with white eggs.

Ms. Lewis: Has anyone figured out why the other number is getting bigger? Kamala noticed that this number [pointing to the first addend] **is getting smaller, but this number** [the second addend] **is getting bigger. Can anyone compare these equations to the eggs? I need you to look at two things at once. I want you to look at the egg carton and then up at the first equation as I keep changing the arrangement of eggs.**

The children watch Ms. Lewis model the first two equations with the "eggs." Squeals of understanding erupt.

Kamala: They go 1, 2, 3, 4, 5 [pointing to the second addend].

Ms. Lewis: What's happening here?

Talia: If this number is going down [first addend], then this number is going up [second addend].

Ms. Lewis: Why?

Talia: We switched them around. We took some different eggs and changed them with different colors.

Maura: You're taking out the blue ones and putting in the white ones.

Talia: Because if you put more of one color, you have less of one color. . . . The white ones are getting bigger because we started with the blue eggs and we put in more white ones. That would make the white ones bigger and the blue ones smaller.

Ms. Lewis: David, why are you nodding your head?

David: Because I know it's right.

....

The goal of this lesson is beyond finding pairs that sum to make 8, writing these arithmetic facts as number sentences, or even identifying patterns. After the students make several observations, the teacher directs them to "look at two things at once," to look at the egg carton *and* the equations as she changes the arrangement of eggs. The students make meaning for the patterns in the symbols by holding in mind the equations along with the corresponding arrangements of eggs: as the addend that corresponds to blue eggs decreases, the addend that corresponds to white eggs increases, because blue eggs are being replaced with white eggs.

Distinguishing Between Different Operations

When students connect symbols with the meanings and actions of the operations, they are better able to distinguish between operations. Without this connection, students may erroneously apply a symbolic pattern describing one operation to another operation. For example, Ms. Lewis' first graders noticed that subtracting 1 from one addend while adding 1 to the other leaves a sum unchanged. Some students might mistakenly extend this rule to claim that $4 \times 5 = 3 \times 6$ (take 1 from the 4 and give it to the 5). Their error lies in applying a rule for addition to another operation without thinking through how the actions of these operations differ.

To visualize why the first graders' addition rule does not apply to multiplication, consider two stories involving groups of pencils. The first represents $4 + 5 = 9$: Janice has 4 pencils and Dean has 5 pencils; between them, they have 9 pencils. The second represents $4 \times 5 = 20$: 4 children each have 5 pencils, altogether sharing 20 pencils. What happens in each case if the 4 and 5 are changed to 3 and 6?

To transform $4 + 5$ to $3 + 6$, imagine Janice gives 1 of her pencils to Dean. Because the total number of pencils is unchanged, we know that $4 + 5 = 3 + 6$.

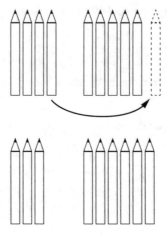

For the multiplication story, begin with 4 children each holding 5 pencils. To change the 4 to 3, imagine that 1 child departs, leaving her pencils behind (so that there are still 20 pencils). Now there are 3 children and 5 extra pencils to distribute. Each child gets an additional pencil, leaving 3 children with 6 pencils each. Because there are now 2 extra pencils, $4 \times 5 \neq 3 \times 6$.

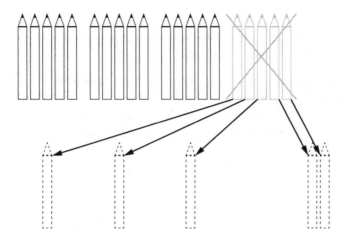

Why are these two situations different? Part of the explanation lies in the meaning of the quantities. In the addition context, the addends and the sum all count the same unit (4 pencils + 5 pencils yields 9 pencils); pencils can be moved from one group to another. In the multiplication context, the factors and product do not count the same units (4 children with 5 pencils per child yields 20 pencils); children cannot be traded for pencils per child.

Elana Winston's third-grade class has been puzzling over this same issue. To focus on this question, Ms. Winston begins a lesson as follows:

$$2 \times 9 = 18 \text{ and } 1 \times 10 = 10, \text{ so } 2 \times 9 \neq 1 \times 10$$

$$BUT\ 2 + 9 = 11 \text{ and } 1 + 10 = 11, \text{ so } 2 + 9 = 1 + 10$$

Ms. Winston: Why is that? Why is it that, in addition, when one part, or addend, goes up by 1 and the other part goes down by that same amount, you end up with the same result? But in multiplication, when you increase one part, or factor, by 1 and decrease the other part by the same amount, you don't get the same result?

Michael: How I know is just that multiplication and addition are totally different things.

Ms. Winston: How are they different?

Paola: For 2 plus 9, you already have the 2, then you add 9. But with the multiplication one, you have 9 twice.

Ms. Winston: **That reminds me of something Felicia wrote on her poster** [reads from a poster created in a previous lesson]: **"One of the numbers is keeping track of how many groups there are, and the other number is keeping track of how many things are in each group."**

Jonny: Can Paola repeat what she said?

Paola: For the addition one, you already have the 2 and then you add 9 to it. In the multiplication one, it's 9 twice. If you were going to turn 2 times 9 into addition, it would be 9 plus 9.

Zarina: When Ingrid and I were talking about this, I was really puzzled. And then she showed me something, and I said, "Oh, my gosh!" But you don't need to get it, because I hardly get it [picks up 2 stacks of cubes]. In addition, you just push those together. [She claps a stack of 9 cubes together with a stack of 2 cubes in a motion showing combining.]

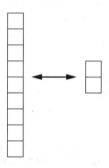

Ingrid [jumping in]: But with multiplication, you're getting another whole row.

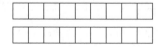

Ms. Winston: **So are you noticing something about what the numbers are doing? Is this like what Paola said, and what Felicia's poster is saying?**

Juan: Like in 2 times 9, the 2 is just telling the 9 how much to do.

Lots of voices: It's just telling the 9 what to do.

Dannah: It's like the boss.

Nicholas: In multiplication, there's two jobs, and in addition, there's only one job.

The class discusses how factors in a multiplication expression have different roles from those of addends. The students compare 2×9 to $2 + 9$, presenting representations with cubes together with verbal descriptions and metaphors, like Dannah's idea that the 2 is the "boss." These students have learned to ask each other to repeat their explanations and consider different metaphors as they work together to understand an idea.

Further questions follow:

....

Nicholas: But then, all of this brings you to, are there other jobs for the numbers in subtraction, and division, too?

Ms. Winston: Interesting question.

Michael: In addition, you just have some numbers and smoosh them together. But everything else, you have one number telling the other what to do.

Josie: I think that in every single one there are different jobs, except for addition.

Dannah: I notice that everything except addition, the numbers have two jobs. Subtraction: Subtract me from your number. Multiplication: It's like a coach says, run around the field 5 laps. 1, 2, 3, 4, 5.

....

When students are introduced to new operations, they learn to recognize the different actions that the operations describe: for example, addition involves joining two groups; multiplication involves joining a given number of groups of fixed size. However, when working with symbols, it is easy for students to forget these meanings and assume that the patterns they notice in one operation also apply to other operations. As students notice each pattern, it is important that they keep in mind the action corresponding to the operation so that they can determine whether a rule that works for one operation applies to another. In Ms. Winston's lesson, students' explanations bring them back to basic representations of addition and multiplication. These explanations elicit new insights about the differences among the operations that can foster further discussions.

Interpreting the Equal Sign

The equal sign, "=," is a very important symbol in algebra. Yet, even though students have been using it for many years by the time they take algebra, the equal sign can still be a source of confusion. This problem can arise if students use and interpret the equal sign in a limited way during the elementary grades.

Elementary students learn to represent the idea, "1 plus 7 make 8" as "$1 + 7 = 8$," as they did in Ms. Lewis' class (pp. 90–92). The word they associate with "=" is *make*. When students see the equal sign used exclusively in this way, they interpret it as meaning "Do the calculation on the left of the equal sign and put the answer on the right of the equal sign." This interpretation of the equal sign can lead students astray.

For example, many students would say the equation $1 + 7 = 2 + 6$ makes no sense. When presented with $1 + 7 = \underline{\quad} + 6$, these students say that the number that goes in the blank should be 8. Frequently students then add 6 to 8 so that their statement reads (incorrectly) $1 + 7 = \underline{8} + 6 = 14$.

Understanding that the equal sign indicates equivalence is essential when students begin to work with algebraic notation. Students who interpret the equal sign as an order to perform a calculation will become confused in algebra, where equations may not require calculation. For example, they would have no way of interpreting such equations as $(a + b)c = ac + bc$ or $3x + 9 = 5x + 5$.

When students understand the equal sign as equivalence, they can interpret equations as statements about relationships or descriptions of situations.

The meaning of the equal sign becomes the subject of discussion in Ruth Callendar's first-grade class. Her students have been working with several contexts for basic addition. When Ms. Callendar asks how to write the notation for the situation they have been discussing, Cory offers $6 = 3 + 3$.

···

Ms. Callendar: Kira, what would that mean, 6 equals 3 plus 3?

Kira: It's the same thing. 6 is the same as 3 plus 3.

Neal: Oh, now I get it.

Ms. Callendar: So Kira says what this means is that 6 is the same as 3 plus 3. Is that true Neal? That 3 plus 3 is 6, they're the same thing?

Neal: Yeah.

Nathaniel: I can't hold my hand up any longer! 6 plus 3 plus 3 doesn't make any sense.

···

Nathaniel reads "=" as "+." Ms. Callendar asks him to read it again, and he says "6 plus 3 plus 3." She asks if that is a plus sign. He says no and reads, "6 equals 3 plus 3," but follows again with "That doesn't make any sense."

Nathaniel's reaction is a common one among students who interpret the equals sign as *make*. To him, the only correct notation is a number, followed by an operation sign, followed by another number, followed by an equal sign, followed by an answer. Cory's suggestion had the symbols in a different order, so it made no sense to Nathaniel, despite Kira's explanation: "6 is the same as 3 plus 3."

Ms. Callendar continues the discussion using images of seesaws and balances. She explains to her students that they can think of the equal sign as the middle of the balance, and that the two quantities are the same when the balance is level. At the end of this discussion, Nathaniel concedes that this idea might be right but adds that it still doesn't make any sense to him.

Six weeks later, questions about the equal sign come up again. The class has solved the following story problem: There were 8 girls on the red climber and 4 boys on the red climber. How many children were on the red climber? Children use different strategies to solve the problem, but all agree the answer is 12. The next problem reads, "At the next recess, there were 4 girls and 8 boys on the climber. How many children were playing on the climber?" All know the answer immediately, and several laugh because the problem is so obvious to them. Ms. Callendar asks for the answer and receives a resounding "12," accompanied by a few giggles.

Children offer these number sentences: $8 + 4 = 12$ and $4 + 8 = 12$. After discussing these for a while, Ms. Callendar writes "$8 + 4 = 4 + 8$" and asks if this makes sense. This time, more students say it does make sense and more can explain that it means that both sides are equivalent. Nathaniel declares confidently, "Yes, because the mathematicians say that you can, and they are the same." Note that although Ms. Callendar has explained equivalence to her first graders, not all of her students accept $8 + 4 = 4 + 8$ as a sensible statement. But with each experience, more students understand the meaning of the equal sign. Through repeated exposure and discussion, all students eventually come to take "$=$" as a symbol of equivalence.

Another teacher, Francis Schwartz, planned to use "Is this equation true?" to explore the commutative property of addition with her first graders. However, each time she began the lesson, she was sidetracked into debate about the meaning of the equal sign. Many students did not yet understand that an equation such as $3 + 4 = 4 + 3$ shows the equivalence of two expressions. Ms. Schwartz realized the importance of clarifying the meaning of the equal sign, but did not want that discussion to usurp her goal of examining equivalent addition expressions. For that reason, she altered the routine. She presented two expressions to the class and asked, "Are these the same amount?"

That change resulted in a very successful lesson. The class concluded that when the order of two addends is changed, the amount remains the same. Toward the end of the lesson, she asked whether there might be a way to write the idea. At this point, someone suggested $3 + 4 = 4 + 3$, and no one in the class objected. Beginning with the idea of commutativity, they found that the "$=$" symbol captured what they wanted to communicate.

It is important that students continue to develop their understanding of the equal sign throughout the elementary grades. Students in Olivia Miller's third-grade class (from Chapter 5) considered equations like $15 + 12 = 17 + 10$. Adio Kweku's fifth graders (from Chapter 4) were asked to articulate a generalization illustrated by $26 \times 12 = 13 \times 24$. Both classes were using the equal sign as a statement of equivalence, and thus becoming more accustomed to its meaning.

Choosing When to Address Issues of Notation

As students investigate the behavior of operations, they need continued support to express new ideas with symbols. Within the complexity of a teaching moment, teachers have to make choices about which issues to pursue. Clarifying meaning may take priority over clarifying notational conventions. Once students have made sense of the mathematical relationships, teachers can help them express those ideas using correct notation.

The work of a student in Alice Kaye's third grade presents several errors. Her class is learning to decompose a factor to help them solve multiplication problems. For example, given the expression 15×6, the 15 can be decomposed into $10 + 5$ to create the equivalent expression $(10 \times 6) + (5 \times 6)$. The ideas in this lesson will later be consolidated as the distributive property of multiplication over addition (see Chapter 9).

Following small-group work, Sierra is convinced there is "an easy way" to generate equivalent expressions and continues to pursue these ideas on her own. After working for a while, Sierra has written:

$15 \times 6 = \underline{\qquad}$

$(14 \times 5 = \underline{\qquad}) + (1 \times 1) = \underline{\qquad}$

$(13 \times 6 = \underline{\qquad}) + (1 \times 0) = \underline{\qquad}$

$(12 \times$

$(11 \times$

$(10 \times$

$(9 \times$

$(8 \times$

$(7 \times$

$(6 \times$

Sierra explains to Ms. Kaye that she is trying to do the same thing she always does when generating equivalent equations. She starts by writing the numbers in descending order and then goes back and fills in the amounts needed to get her back to the original number. When she tried to do this with 15×6, she got to the second line, $(13 \times 6) + (1 \times 0)$, and it just did not look right. She cannot figure out what went wrong.

There are several problems with Sierra's work. For one, she places an equation in parentheses within another equation. Although it may be clear what Sierra intends, the first equal sign in each of the first two lines is incorrect.

Also, Sierra has misapplied a rule that works for addition. Whereas it is true that $(14 + 5) + (1 + 1) = 15 + 6$, when the operation shifts to multiplication, $(14 \times 5) + (1 \times 1) \neq 15 \times 6$. However, Sierra seems satisfied with this formulation. It is not until she tries to generate the next line that $(13 \times 6) + (1 \times 0)$ doesn't look right to her.

Faced with Sierra's page, Ms. Kaye must decide what to work on. For now, she decides to ignore the incorrect use of the equal sign to focus on the meaning of multiplication. She brings Sierra's attention to the context the class had been working with for 15×6: the number of legs on 15 insects. Ms. Kaye describes what happens.

I invited her to talk through the story context for her first expression, $(14 \times 5) + (1 \times 1)$. She wasn't sure what I meant, so I provided the story: "When you did this first part, 14×5, it was like figuring out how much it would be to have 5 legs on each of 14 insects. Then, the other part, the 1×1, was like taking one leg from one of the other insects.

Sierra was puzzled for a moment and then told me, "But that wouldn't be right." She started to change things and eventually the equation read $(14 \times 6) + (1 \times 6) =$ ___. She responded well to reembedding the work in the context of the original problem in order to hold onto what was happening.

Then she went to the next line, $(13 \times 6) + (1 \times 0)$, but she couldn't bring the story context back without my support. As I walked her through this one, attaching the story about insects to her numbers, she lit up and said, "So, I have to keep the 6 every time, right? I always have to have 6 legs, and I always have to have 15 insects." I then left her to work on it some more by herself.

When I returned, Sierra had continued her sequence of equations, and her page now looked like this:

$15 \times 6 =$ ___

$(14 \times 6 =$ ___ $) + (1 \times 6) =$ ___

$(13 \times 6 =$ ___ $) + (2 \times 6) =$ ___

$(12 \times 6 =$ ___ $) + (3 \times 6) =$ ___

$(11 \times 6 =$ ___ $) + (4 \times 6) =$ ___

$(10 \times 6 =$ ___ $) + (5 \times 6) =$ ___

$(9 \times 6 =$ ___ $) + (6 \times 6) =$ ___

When I asked Sierra about this work, she was feeling pretty satisfied with herself.

Sierra's initial effort presented several errors. Ms. Kaye prioritized the issues and chose to bring Sierra's attention back to the meaning of multiplication in order to think through how to maintain equivalence when one factor of an expression is decomposed. On another occasion, with Sierra's understanding solid on these ideas, Ms. Kaye can work with her on the correct use of the equal sign.

MAKING MEANING FOR ALGEBRAIC NOTATION

In the preceding episodes, students use arithmetic symbols to convey particular instances of a generalization. For example, Ms. Callendar's first graders use "$4 + 8 = 8 + 4$" to express their understanding that reversing the order of addends does not change the sum (the commutative property of addition). Ms. Kaye's third grader, Sierra, writes a sequence of multiplication expressions equivalent to 15×6, based on an idea that will later be consolidated as the distributive property of multiplication over addition. The introduction of algebraic symbols—specifically, using letters to stand for unspecified numbers—allows students to write generalizations concisely. Read the following cases to see students using algebraic symbols to represent generalizations that arise as they work in arithmetic.

Using Variables to Express a Generalization

In Marlena Diaz's fifth-grade classroom, students are identifying addition expressions equal to 32 and have written the following:

$$30 + 2$$

$$29 + 3$$

$$28 + 4$$

$$27 + 5$$

Students say that this sequence is a specific case of a generalization—you can subtract 1 from one addend and add 1 to the other, and the total stays the same. To justify their claim, they use cubes to show how one expression can be transformed into the next, without adding any more cubes or taking any away.

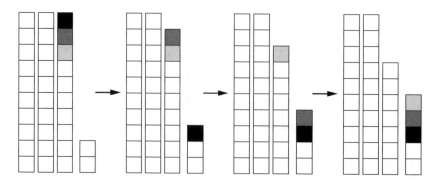

Students argue, "Since all the numbers are made up of ones, we can just move all those ones around."

Because the students are clear about the statement and argument, Ms. Diaz decides that symbolic notation would provide another representation for them to use to think about this idea.

· ·

Ms. Diaz: It seems that you all are thinking that this is true about all numbers and you are making convincing arguments. I wonder if we could write a sentence that wouldn't use numbers to show what is happening. Could we call these numbers up here on the chart just some numbers?

Will: We could write letters for them. Like *n* for number, like *n one* and *n two*.

Ms. Diaz: That's a great idea. One thing that mathematicians do sometimes is use different letters so they don't get confused. How about if we use *a* and *b*?

Jonah: We could write *a* plus *b* equals a number.

Ms. Diaz: So let's use Jonah's idea and try to write down what we did to the two quantities. What are we doing to the *a* and the *b* in this pattern?

Ms. Diaz records a *above the first addend and* b *above the second addend:*

$$a \quad b$$

$$30 + 2$$

$$29 + 3$$

$$28 + 4$$

$$27 + 5$$

Kathryn: We can write *a* plus *b* is the same as *a* take 1 away and *b* add 1 to it.

Ms. Diaz [recording $a + b = (a - 1) + (b + 1)$]: **How does this match what Kathryn said and what we did with the cubes?**

Reynold: We take 1 away like here in the pattern . . . one goes up and one goes down.

Ms. Diaz next asks students to think about the cubes again and consider moving more than 1 cube from one stack to the other. Several students point out that they could move any number of cubes from one stack to the other and maintain the same total. Ms. Diaz asks if that idea could be shown with the notation.

Adena: We could write lots of them and change the numbers. *[Adena is suggesting they write a series of equations, $a + b = (a - 1) + (b + 1)$; $a + b = (a - 2) + (b + 2)$, and so forth.]*

Will: Or we could write, add any and take any away.

Jonah: We could use another letter.

Ms. Diaz: What do you all think?

Adena: Put a *c*. Put *a* plus *b* equals *c*.

Jonah: But put the *c* where the 1 is.

Ms. Diaz [*recording:* $a + b = (a - c) + (b + c)$]**: Do you mean like this, put the *c* where the 1 is? What does this mean now?**

Reynold: See, the *c* is the cubes you move around to the other side.

In this lesson, students begin to use algebraic notation. With careful guidance, they represent a generalization they had already articulated and demonstrated with cubes. Students offer various suggestions. (Will suggested using "*n one* and *n two*," and Adena thought they should write "*a + b = c.*") The teacher chooses to follow those suggestions that lead to the most concise algebraic statement:

$$a + b = (a - c) + (b + c)$$

Through exposure to the use of variables, students begin to learn the conventions of notation. In particular, their statement applies the convention that the same letter is used to indicate the same number throughout the equation. They are also learning how parentheses are used to indicate the order of operations: One pair of parentheses captures the action of taking an amount from the first addend; the other pair, the action of adding the same amount to the second addend.[1]

Significantly, the students developed meaning for the symbols "+," "−," and "=" in earlier years. In this context, "+" is associated with the image of joining cubes, "−" with removal of cubes, and "=" signifies that the same number of cubes is represented by $a + b$ and by $(a - c) + (b + c)$. With these meanings firmly established, students can interpret the new symbols, the variables, in terms of the idea the statement represents. For example, Reynold specifies that "*c* is the cubes you move around to the other side."

For another example, consider again Alice Kaye's third-grade class. Students are given the following problems and are asked to state what they notice.

---

1 In this example, the statement is still true without the parentheses: $a + b = a - c + b + c$. However, this changes the order in which the operations are performed and, thus, no longer captures the intent of the students.

$7 + 5 = 12$	$7 + 5 = 12$
$7 + 6 = \underline{}$	$8 + 5 = \underline{}$
$9 + 4 = 13$	$9 + 4 = 13$
$9 + 5 = \underline{}$	$10 + 4 = \underline{}$

Working together, the class articulates, "In addition, if you increase one of the addends by 1 and keep the other addend(s) the same, then the sum will also increase by 1."

Ms. Kaye asks her students how they would convince someone that this statement is true. Students work in groups creating posters showing their ideas using story contexts, pictures, models, or examples. Review of all the posters generates lively discussion. Helen comments, "You know, all of these sound exactly the same. Even though everybody did something different, really everybody is showing the same thing."

At this point, Ms. Kaye introduces algebraic notation. She says, "You know how we're all struggling with all the words we're using—first number, second number. There is a way we can capture this idea. See what you think of this."

She writes on the board:

$$\text{If } a + b = c$$

$$\text{then } (a + 1) + b = c + 1$$

$$\text{and } a + (b + 1) = c + 1$$

Some students are confused and object. But most are able to see their recent work reflected in these statements, saying, "Oh, that makes so much sense!"

Investigations in Ms. Kaye's class continue with further opportunities for students to think through how to represent generalizations with algebraic notation. However, expressing generalizations algebraically is not the end point Ms. Kaye has in mind for her students. She does not insist that all students use algebraic notation but offers it as another avenue for students to clarify and enhance their understanding of general claims.

The following characteristics of these fifth- and third-grade episodes indicate appropriate conditions for the introduction of algebraic notation:

- The students have articulated a claim.

- The students have had opportunity to examine and justify the claim.

- The teacher is clear about how the claim can be represented algebraically and judges that this notation is close enough to students' articulations of the claim as to be potentially within their grasp.

- Students have a chance to connect the algebraic statement to the ideas and representations on which they have been working.

Algebraic Notation Is Not an End Point

The fact that a student can write a generalization in algebraic notation does not mean he/she knows all there is to know about that statement. Work on the idea must continue, using words, diagrams or manipulatives, different kinds of numbers, and, where appropriate, returning to algebraic notation.

Consider the work of a group of sixth-graders who had noticed and verbalized the following: If two numbers are multiplied, you can double one factor and halve the other without changing the product. The teacher, Jeannette McCorkle, helped them write out the generalization as $a \times b = (a \times 2) \times (b/2)$. Then they extended the claim to include multiplying and dividing by any factor, expressing this broader generalization as $a \times b = (a \times c) \times (b/c)$. However, writing the statement in algebraic notation was not the final step. Over the next several weeks, the class continued to encounter this idea, always in the context of whole numbers. In the following episode, they recognize the idea in the context of multiplying decimals.

Ms. McCorkle posts the following:

$$25 \times 1 = 2.5 \times 10$$

$$25 \times 10 = 2.5 \times \underline{\quad}$$

$$25 \times 100 = .25 \times \underline{\quad}$$

$$25 \times .1 = 2.5 \times \underline{\quad}$$

$$25 \times .01 = .25 \times \underline{\quad}$$

⋯⋯⋯⋯⋯⋯⋯⋯⋯⋯⋯⋯⋯⋯⋯⋯⋯⋯⋯⋯

Ms. McCorkle: So look at this *[first equation]* for a minute and when you have decided if that is a true equation, without calculating, when you have a strategy for determining whether that is true, raise your hand and let me know.

Elspeth: I'm not sure if this is right at all, but if 2.5 is timesed by 10, it means moving the decimal over one, and that is the same thing as 25 × 1.

Althea: Well, 2.5 is 10 times smaller than 25, and 10 is 10 times bigger than 1.

Billy: 2.5 times 10, if you multiply it by 10, you move it one to the right, so you're looking at 25 and 25.

Lucy: I would think of 2.5 times 10 as 2 tens and a half a 10, which is 25, so you have 25 and 25.

Althea: This is like the problems we did before but *a* is divided by 10 and *b* is multiplied by 10.

Ms. McCorkle designed the lesson to work on difficulties in decimal computation. Specifically, her intention was to make sure her students were thinking about "moving the decimal point" as a multiplication or division by a power of 10, not simply as a mechanical process. As she sets her students to work in small groups, she keeps in mind Althea's observation, knowing she will return to it.

In their small groups, some students exhibit the mechanical methods that concern her. To solve the last problem, one student says:

I'm sort of like, 25 times .01 equals .25 times . . . , it has to be 1, because to get .25 you have to move the decimal over two, so then to get to 1 you have to move it two the other way.

Ms. McCorkle does not want her students to simply memorize rules for moving decimal points. Instead, she wants them to reason about multiplication and division. She brings the class together to focus on this.

Ms. McCorkle: You're looking at a number-of-decimal-places relationship, and I want to expand that and talk about how one factor has been multiplied and another factor has been divided. The number of decimal places is just one way of talking about how factors have been altered.

Elspeth: It's not just about the decimal point, it's about multiplying and dividing the numbers.

Ms. McCorkle: Exactly. I want to remind you about the pattern we were looking at last week and the week before, when Althea suggested that $a \times b = 2a \times \frac{1}{2} b$, and Gabe suggested that $a \times b = ac \times \frac{b}{c}$. Althea, how was 25×1 changed into 2.5×10?

Althea: The first factor was divided by 10 and the second factor was multiplied by 10.

Ms. McCorkle: That's right. The decimal moved back means divided by 10, so to maintain this equality, what should happen to this factor?

Most students: Multiply by 10.

Althea: And it's still $a \times b = ac \times \frac{b}{c}$.

Previously, the class had noticed and articulated a generalization and represented it using variables. Introducing decimals allows students to extend their understanding of the algebraic statement, and the compact notation helps them to make explicit connections between operating with whole numbers and decimals.

Several points can be made about the use of notation in this lesson:

- Students are challenged to think about the connection between moving the decimal point and multiplying and dividing by powers of 10.

- The class comes to see that the generalization they have articulated for whole numbers, $a \times b = ac \times \frac{b}{c}$, also applies to decimals. In this lesson, a and b might be decimal numbers and c might be 10 or 100 or any other power of 10.

- More generally, they begin to see that operating with decimal numbers requires no new set of rules; rather, generalizations they have made for whole numbers can be applied to calculations with decimals.

ISSUES IN USING ALGEBRAIC NOTATION

You have seen the power and accessibility of algebraic notation for students learning to articulate generalizations about the behavior of operations. However, teachers introducing algebraic notation to elementary students must choose carefully when to employ these symbolic representations and understand the difficulties inherent in their use. Students need time to learn the correct use of letter notation just as they do to interpret arithmetic symbols and the equal sign. Teachers are often unaware of issues students face when they begin to use algebraic notation.

Algebraic symbols have different conventions from those of numbers. The following sections provide examples of issues arising as students encounter this notation. Teachers must be aware of these new and unfamiliar aspects of the notation when they choose to wade into the territory of algebraic notation.

Example 1: Not All Generalizations Can Be Represented by Algebraic Notation

The school's math coach is visiting Judy Mack's third-grade classroom while students discuss multiplying by 10. The students say that to multiply by 10, all you have to do is "attach zero to the number. Say you have 49 times 10. You attach a 0 to 49 to get 490."

During the course of the school year, Ms. Mack has often helped her students represent general claims using algebraic notation. Because the students are clearly articulating a generalization, Ms. Mack suggests they try to write it algebraically. She writes, "$n \times 10 =$," but feels unsure how to proceed. She moves forward, writing, "$n \times 10 = n0$," and turns around to her coach with a questioning look. The coach suggests that she erase the statement; this generalization does not lend itself to algebraic expression.

Implicit in the place value system is a series of multiplications and additions. Each digit of a number is multiplied by a power of 10. The value of the number is the sum of the products: $5,932 = (5 \times 1,000) + (9 \times 100) + (3 \times 10) + (2 \times 1)$. The place value system conveys a great deal of information in a compact form, allowing us to represent extremely large quantities with very few symbols. But the conventions of algebra differ from those of place value. For example, the placement of two symbols next to each other conveys multiplication in algebraic notation. That is, ab means $a \times b$—if $a = 3$ and $b = 2$, then $ab = 6$. On the other hand, when the symbols 3 and 2 are written next to each other in place value notation as 32, the meaning is $(3 \times 10) + (2 \times 1)$. If $n = 49$, $n0$ does not denote 490 in algebraic notation, because $n0$ means $n \times 0$, which is equal to 0. There is no straightforward way to use algebraic notation to communicate "attach 0 to the right of the number."

Similarly, when Ms. McCorkle's students were multiplying decimals, one student suggested: $a.b \times c = ab \times .c$. This student was thinking of ab as the number $(a \times 10) + (b \times 1)$, $a.b$ as $(a \times 1) + (b \times .1)$, and $.c$ as $c \times .1$, where a, b, and c take on the values 1, 2, 3, 4, 5, 6, 7, 8, or 9. (It's not clear if she would allow a or b to equal 0.) In terms of the student's experience, the invented notation is reasonable. However, in algebraic notation, a and b represent numbers of any size, and ab means $a \times b$. The symbols "$a.b$" and "$.c$" (inserting decimal points among the letters) have no meaning in conventional algebraic notation.

As students begin to use algebraic notation, they may try to apply it to represent the ideas of place value, as in the two examples above. In cases like these, teachers will have to choose the most important focus for instruction, just as Ms. Kaye did when confronted with Sierra's misuse of the equal sign (pp. 98–99). Should the focus be on clarifying, representing, and justifying the student's mathematical idea, on correcting the incorrect notation, or on both? To make these decisions, teachers must recognize the limitations of algebraic notation and determine when and how to help students become familiar with its conventions.

Example 2: Letters Are Not Always Variables

Letters are used in different ways at different times in elementary mathematics. Sometimes letters do not represent variables subject to the conventions of algebraic notation. For example, letters may be used as labels. Students working to answer the question, "There are 7 peas and carrots on your plate. How many peas and how many carrots are there?" may find a variety of solutions and use the following notation:

$$3P + 4C$$

$$5P + 2C$$

$$6P + 1C$$

These first graders are using letters as labels, not variables. P does not represent a number; instead it is short for *peas*. $3P$ stands for 3 peas. If P were a variable, $3P$ would mean "multiply 3 by whatever number P stands for." For example, if $P = 3$, then $3P = 9$.

Students may also use letters as a form of shorthand. While investigating odd and even numbers, students often make generalizations such as, "The sum of two even numbers is even; the sum of two odd numbers is even; and the sum of an even number and an odd number is odd." They may write these statements using E to represent any even number and O to represent any odd number:

$$E + E = E$$

$$O + O = E$$

$$O + E = O$$

With this use of notation, for the statement "$E + E = E$," each E can be any even number; the first E might equal 2, the second, 4, and the third would equal 6: $2 + 4 = 6$. While E and O *do* represent unspecified numbers, they are not being used as algebraic variables. In an algebraic expression, a variable stands for the same number every time it appears. Used as a variable, E cannot stand for 2, 4, and 6 in the same equation; the only value of E that makes the equation true is 0: $0 + 0 = 0$.

Teachers need to be aware of these uses of letters in mathematics and understand that not all letters are algebraic variables.

Example 3: x Is Sometimes Less Than 0

Issues of understanding also arise when algebraic notation is used in ways counter to students' expectations. Students encountering negative numbers frequently notice regularities in their behavior and articulate generalizations. But they may get stuck when they try to put their ideas into algebraic notation. One difficulty arises because x does not always represent a positive number and $-x$ does not always represent a negative number. By definition, $-x$ is the additive inverse of x. That is, $-x$ is the number that, when added to x, results in 0: $x + (-x) = 0$. If $x = 2$, then $-x = -2$, but if $x = -2$, then $-x = 2$.

In Ms. McCorkle's class, the students are exploring the generalization $a \times b = (a \div 2) \times (b \times 2)$. Because a and b can take on negative values, the single statement covers *all* positive whole numbers and fractions, *and* covers the case when a and/or b are negative. Many students at first think that negative numbers require a different statement, that you would write $-a \times b = (-a \div 2) \times (b \times 2)$ for the same generalization applied to negative numbers. These students are assuming that a stands for a positive value, and that to communicate that the first factor may be negative, the variable needs a negative sign. They still need to learn that variables can take on all the values on the number line.

IN CONCLUSION . . .

Some may ask, why not introduce algebraic notation as soon as students begin to verbalize generalizations? After all, it is often much easier to write the statement of a generalization using symbolic notation than in an English sentence. The question to ask before introducing algebraic notation is whether the notation will enhance the meaning of an idea for students. As they represent a generalization in different ways, are students connecting these representations with the meaning and behavior of the operations? Does the algebraic representation of the idea offer them new insights or clarity in communication? Or do students memorize patterns of symbols without associating them with meaning?

Answers to these questions differ from class to class and claim to claim. For example, although the notation $x + y = y + x$ may be accessible to primary-grade students who have worked on the corresponding generalization, notation for other claims may be less accessible. A second- or third-grade class working with a sequence of equivalent subtraction expressions might formulate the following rule: If you add something to the first number, you have to add the same amount to the subtracted number to keep the same result. However, algebraic notation for this idea, $a - b = (a + n) - (b + n)$, may be difficult for them to follow and may not add to their understanding of the generalization.

By judiciously choosing when to introduce algebraic notation, teachers help students in younger grades make meaning for algebraic symbols. When students have already articulated a generalization and illustrated it with various representations, they can use the symbols to express an idea they already understand. Introducing algebraic notation in this way prepares students for later grades and also offers another representation of generalizations about operations.

In the next chapter, we return to considering students' representation-based proof, with a focus on how students decide to which numbers their claims apply and how they justify their claims when they consider new classes of numbers, such as fractions or negative numbers. This chapter also includes further examples in which students incorporate algebraic notation into their work. ∎

FOCUS QUESTIONS

LEARNING ALGEBRAIC NOTATION: LOOKING AT TWO THINGS AT ONCE

1. **Chapter 7 includes episodes in which students begin to develop meaning for symbols. As you read this chapter, you may have been reminded of your own past experiences with algebraic symbols.**

   • How are the ideas presented in this chapter similar to or different from your own experience as a learner?

   • What are the implications of this work for you as a teacher?

2. **Consider the classroom episode in Chapter 7 from Ms. Lewis' class.**

   • What mathematical idea is the class working on in this episode?

   • What is it that Talia contributes to the conversation?

   • Examine the questions posed by Ms. Lewis. Describe their content and impact.

3. **Chapter 7 includes examples of students working to make sense of the equal sign.**

   • What kinds of understandings or misunderstandings about the use of the equal sign have you seen in your students' work?

   • What math tasks might you pose or questions might you ask to help your students make sense of this symbol?

4. **Consider the classroom episode from Ms. Kaye's work with Sierra.**

   • Trace the discussion as the conversation unfolds by explaining the thinking of the student in the case.

5. **Consider the students' ideas in Marlena Diaz's episode as the class works together to develop a symbolic expression for a familiar general claim.**

   • What is it that Will, Jonah, Kathryn, Adena, and Reynold each contribute to the discussion?

   • Examine the questions posed by Ms. Diaz. Describe their content and impact.

6. **Chapter 7 also includes a section titled, Issues in Using Algebraic Notation, and a conclusion that suggests what teachers should consider as they try to decide on the usefulness of algebraic symbols for their own class.**

   • What is your reaction to the issues that are raised in the issues section?

   • What are your current thoughts about introducing symbolic notation to your students?

8

Developing Mathematical Arguments

What Is the Domain?

Representations such as manipulatives, diagrams, and story contexts not only are useful for solving particular problems but also can serve as a basis for reasoning about the behavior of the operations. Chapter 5 introduced the use of representation-based proofs for generalizations about an infinite class of numbers. This chapter continues the discussion of representation-based proof and offers further examples of student proofs.

It also addresses the questions: What is the domain of numbers the students consider? That is, what set of numbers is included in the proof? The chapter presents examples from first to fifth grade, illustrating how students' understanding of number expands. As students' sights extend from whole numbers to negative numbers and fractions, how do their proofs change?

CRITERIA FOR REPRESENTATION-BASED PROOF

Alina Martinez's fifth graders provide a review of representation-based proof. After seeing several examples of equivalent multiplication expressions—$30 \times 2 = 15 \times 4$,

24 × 3 = 12 × 6, 18 × 14 = 9 × 28—and after several attempts at articulating a generalization, the students state:

> *When multiplying two numbers, if you double one number and take half of the other, the product stays the same.*

Ms. Martinez then gives the class the challenge:

> *Can you come up with a representation that shows this will always be true, no matter what numbers you start with? Make a picture, draw a model, but don't use any particular numbers.*

The students create a variety of representations, such as the following poster, which was created by Trish and Emily. Trish and Emily's proof is based on showing that specific rectangles have the same area. They present three drawings, each showing a step of their proof. The first rectangle is labeled "original," and has dimensions T and E. Its area represents the product, $T \times E$. The second drawing shows the original divided into two congruent rectangles, each with dimensions $\frac{1}{2}T$ and E. In the third drawing, the two congruent rectangles are rearranged with one placed above the other. This creates a new rectangle with dimensions $\frac{1}{2}T$ and $E \times 2$. No area has been lost or added, so the rectangle of dimensions $\frac{1}{2}T$ and $2E$ has the same area as the rectangle with dimensions T and E. This implies that $T \times E = \frac{1}{2}T \times 2E$.

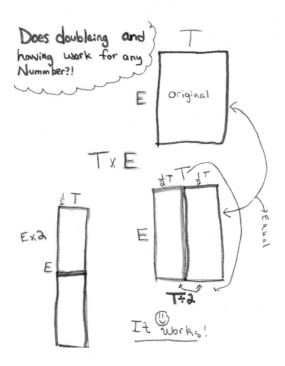

Trish and Emily's reasoning meets the criteria for representation-based proof that were laid out in Chapter 5:

1. *The meaning of the operations involved in the claim is represented in the diagram.* Trish and Emily represent the products $T \times E$ and $\frac{1}{2}T \times 2E$ as the areas of rectangles with dimensions equal to the factors. $\frac{1}{2}T$ (that is, $\frac{1}{2} \times T$) is represented as $\frac{1}{2}$ the length of the segment equal to T. $2E$ ($2 \times E$) is represented as $2 \times$ the length of the segment equal to E.

2. *The representation can accommodate a class of instances.* The dimensions of the original rectangle, T and E, can represent any positive numbers.

3. *The conclusion of the claim follows from the structure of the representation; that is, the representation shows why the statement must be true.* Because the second rectangle can be created by rearranging pieces of the first rectangle, no matter what positive values T and E take on, the area of a rectangle with dimensions $T \times E$ will be equal to the area of a rectangle with dimensions $\frac{1}{2}T$ and $2E$. The product $T \times E$ is equal to the product $\frac{1}{2}T \times 2E$.

As you read the following student-devised proofs, focus on criterion 2. What class of numbers do the students consider?

FIRST AND SECOND GRADERS CONSIDER "VERY LARGE NUMBERS" AND "INFINITY"

As Ruth Callendar's first graders learned about addition and subtraction, they started to notice relationships among problems. Sometimes they would use the answer from one problem to figure out the answer to another.

In early June, Ms. Callendar challenges her students to articulate and explore the generalization embedded in two related problems. She intentionally keeps the numbers small and chooses a combination of addends in the first problem that the children can easily compute. She believes that most of the class can solve the second problem by using the answer to the first problem.

1. *On Saturday, there were 5 girls and 5 boys in the pool. How many children were in the pool?*

2. *On Sunday, there were 5 girls and 6 boys in the pool. Can you use the answer from the other story to help you figure out how many children were in the pool on Sunday?*

Ms. Callendar then poses questions designed to address whether the students can do more than use the result of the first problem to solve the second. Can they also talk about why it works?

Please draw a diagram that shows how knowing 5 + 5 = 10 helps you figure out 5 + 6. Why does it work? Will it work with really big numbers, too?

The students work on the tasks and think hard about the questions. All produce correct answers to the word problems, and many explain in writing the rule they are using—expressing themselves as best they can with their first-grade knowledge of spelling.

Marjorie: I no 5 + 5 = 10 and if you add one more it is six. And ten ples one is 11 so 5 + 6 = 11.

Melanie: I yousd a Helper 5 + 5 = 10 you just put 1 more on and it eqls 11.

Emma: 5 + 6 = 11 I now that 5 + 5 = 10 so the number after 10 is the anser.

Only one child, Antoine, produces a diagram demonstrating how the two story problems are related. He draws the children in the problems and, with help from Ms. Callendar, labels the different components. The 5 girls and 5 boys to the left of the vertical line represent the first story problem, labeled "Saturday." To represent the second story problem, he incorporates the first representation, adding 1 boy to the right of the vertical line. In Antoine's picture, all children in the pool on Saturday come back on Sunday and 1 additional boy joins them. Adding 1 boy increases the total by 1.

Please draw a diagram that shows how knowing 5+5=10 helps you to figure out 5+6. Why does it work?

Saturday   Sunday

Girls →

Boys →   boy

Will it work with really big numbers too?

Yes

Antoine's diagram meets the first and third criteria for representation-based proof. He has represented addition as the joining of sets (criterion 1). The conclusion—adding 1 boy increases the total number of children by 1—follows from the structure of his representation (criterion 3). Antoine does not explain how the representation can accommodate a class of instances (criterion 2). However, he answers yes to Ms. Callendar's final question, "Will it work with really big numbers, too?"

During the class discussion, Ms. Callendar takes the students through an argument similar to Antoine's, using blue cubes to represent the 5 girls and green cubes to represent the 5 boys that came on Saturday and the 1 boy that joined them on Sunday. All participate in explaining the argument, agreeing that it shows that when $5 + 5$ is changed to $5 + 6$, the total changes from 10 to 11.

Ms. Callendar is interested to see if her students can generalize the finding that adding 1 to an addend increases the sum by 1.

··

Ms. Callendar: OK. So let me ask you another hard question then. Is it going to work with really big numbers?

Several students: Yes.

Ms. Callendar: So let's say I tell you something. Let's say I told you that 15 plus 5 equals 20. If I told you this, could you use it to figure out 15 plus 6?

Several voices: Yeah, 21.

Melanie: 21, because you just add 1 more on like with the boys and the girls.

Ms. Callendar: Like you just add 1 more on, like the boys and the girls. So it works with numbers that are a little bigger. Is it going to work with numbers that are even bigger?

Class [many answers at once]**:** Yes. No.

Ms. Callendar: If I tell you 26 plus 3; let's figure it out: 27, 28, 29. What does it equal?

All: 29.

Ms. Callendar: So would that help you figure out what 26 plus 4 equals?

Many: Yes, 30.

Melanie: Because you just do the same thing.

Ms. Callendar: And what is that same thing you're doing?

Marjorie: You're adding 1 on.

Ms. Callendar: You're adding on 1 to what, Emma?

Emma: To the other number.

Ms. Callendar: You're adding 1 on to the other number, and what does that do to the answer? How does that change the answer, Cindy?

Cindy: It changes it 'cause it's 1 higher.

Ms. Callendar: It changes it because it's 1 higher. So, is it always going to change the answer if you change one of the numbers?

A few yeses. Others are quiet.

....

As is typical for students beginning work on generalization, Ms. Callendar's class needs help to articulate the rule they are discussing. When Ms. Callendar asks, "And what is that same thing you're doing?" individual students offer parts of the claim: "You're adding 1 on," "To the other number," "It changes [the answer] 'cause it's 1 higher." They correctly answer that, because $15 + 5 = 20$, it must be true that $15 + 6 = 21$. Melanie states, "Because you just add 1 more on, like with the boys and the girls," and "Because you just do the same thing." The story context allows students to create images for the pairs of addition expressions that they can apply to specific examples.

However, when Ms. Callendar asks whether the claim works with numbers that are even bigger, and whether it works with all numbers, the class's response is more tentative. Although some students answer yes, some answer no or don't respond at all.

At this age, many students are beginning to develop a sense of the consistency of the number system. They are aware there are numbers larger than those they work with, but are just coming to realize that these numbers are accessed by continually adding 1. They will eventually learn that that there are numbers corresponding to groups of objects too large to imagine, although most have not yet encountered the idea that numbers extend infinitely. The sorts of questions Ms. Callendar poses challenge students to think about what happens when operating with numbers larger than those with which they are familiar.

Isabel Hazelton's second-grade classroom provides a glimpse of students first encountering the possibility of reasoning about an infinite set. The Number of the Day routine has brought their attention to different ways to create equivalent expressions. For example, starting with any addition expression, then subtracting 1 from one addend and adding 1 to the other will produce an equivalent expression: $12 + 7$ becomes $11 + 8$. Adding 1 to both terms of any subtraction expression also produces an equivalent expression: $20 - 1$ becomes $21 - 2$.

The students have also noticed that for any number they have tried, they can find *all* the equivalent addition expressions.[1] But today, as the class lists addition and subtraction expressions equal to 19, Brandon notices something special about subtraction.

....

1 Because these second graders are working in the domain of whole numbers, there is a finite set of addition combinations for any given sum.

....

Brandon: I'm noticing something. Subtraction can go on forever.

Ms. Hazelton: What do you think about that?

His classmates respond with giggles and "yeahs."

Connor: With subtraction patterns, it just keeps going and going and going.

Ms. Hazelton: What keeps it going?

Connor: All the numbers. It keeps going on by 1. Like 12 minus 0 and 13 minus 1; it just keeps going on by 1.

Klaus: That's one thing that I'm wondering about. Why does it happen? 'Cause at my house, I've done it and it keeps going and going and it never stops.

Marissa: Well, you could go on to like a zillion and infinity.

....

For these students, the question "Will this always work?" has a different meaning. They see that numbers go on without end, that the process of adding 1 can go on indefinitely. Their comments imply that, no matter how large two numbers are, if their difference is 12, adding 1 to each number will result in another subtraction expression with a difference of 12.

Many students experience the wonder these students express when they realize that numbers extend infinitely. Some students question the possibility of proof when they realize that there are numbers that are much larger than what they can imagine: "How can you make a claim about all numbers, when you can't test all numbers? Maybe there is some very large number out there for which it is not true." The power of mathematics is that claims for an infinite class *can* be proven. The next section provides examples of students who successfully prove claims about all whole numbers.

THIRD GRADERS MAKE CLAIMS ABOUT ALL (WHOLE) NUMBERS

As you read the next episode, consider how the students address the question, "How can you make a claim about numbers when numbers extend infinitely?"

Adding 1 to an Addend

Alice Kaye brings her third graders' attention to the same generalization that Ruth Callendar's first graders were working on. She gives the students a set of problems and asks them what they notice.[2]

---

2 Chapter 7 presented the same lesson from Ms. Kaye's class to illustrate the introduction of algebraic notation after students articulated the generalization and presented their proofs. In this chapter, we look more closely at the students' proofs.

$7 + 5 = 12$	$7 + 5 = 12$
$7 + 6 = \underline{\ \ }$	$8 + 5 = \underline{\ \ }$
$9 + 4 = 13$	$9 + 4 = 13$
$9 + 5 = \underline{\ \ }$	$10 + 4 = \underline{\ \ }$

The class notices regularity in these calculations and works together to make a complete statement of the generalization:

> *In addition, if you increase one of the addends by 1 and keep the other addend(s) the same, then the sum will also increase by 1.*

Ms. Kaye asks the class how they would convince someone that this is true. Groups create posters that illustrate their ideas. Some students struggle to hold onto the generalization as they draw pictures, offer story contexts, and provide examples. The idea is one that they can apply fluently, but it's still a challenge to prove it.

Working on their proofs helps individual students come to believe the claim and understand it more deeply. Their posters and discussion indicate that, unlike the first graders, they *are* thinking about numbers as extending infinitely. These students are developing an understanding of the infinite set of whole numbers.

Consider Nathan, Todd, Jonah, and Carl's poster. In discussion they declare, "If it works for numbers of this size, it must always work!"

$$9,000,000\ 000,000,000,000,000,000,000,000,000,000 +$$
$$9,000,000,000\ 000,000,000,000,000,000,000,000,001 = 18 \text{ decillion and } 1$$

9 decillion and $2 + 9$ decillion $= 18$ decillion and 2

These boys know they can keep writing zeros to get larger and larger numbers and they learn that the number they have written is called 9 decillion. Furthermore, they have confidence that addition behaves the same with numbers greater than they can imagine as with numbers they work with every day.

Their poster provides an example that *illustrates* the claim but is not a proof. In contrast, consider Megan's poster.

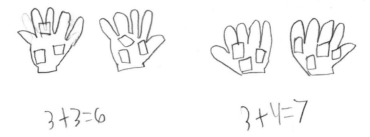

$$3+3=6 \qquad\qquad 3+4=7$$

At the left of Megan's poster are two hands, each holding 3 cubes. On the right are the same two hands, with an additional cube held in one hand. The total number of cubes increases from 6 to 7. At first, it might seem that Megan has also provided only an example.

Like Antoine's picture, Megan's poster satisfies two of the criteria for representation-based proof. She represents addition as joining sets of cubes (criterion 1). And she demonstrates why the claim is true—once a cube is added to one hand, the total number of cubes in the two hands increases by 1 (criterion 3). But it is her verbal description explaining how her picture can accommodate all whole numbers (criterion 2) that makes it a representation-based proof:

> *The picture could be used for any numbers, not just 3 and 4. I could have started with anything in one hand, and then anything else in the other hand, and put them together. If I got 1 more thing in either hand, the total would always only go up by 1.*

Although the poster provides a picture of how 3 + 3 and 3 + 4 are related, it also provides an image applicable to any addition expression. Megan tells the class that any number of cubes may be held in each of the two hands before adding a single cube to one hand. The total number of cubes in the two hands must then increase by 1. Thus, the poster, *together with Megan's explanation*, satisfies criterion 2. Her words tell us how the picture can be viewed to accommodate all whole numbers.

As described in Chapter 7, Ms. Kaye ends the lesson by showing her class the generalization in algebraic notation:

$$\text{If } a + b = c$$

$$\text{then } (a + 1) + b = c + 1$$

$$\text{and } a + (b + 1) = c + 1$$

Some students recognize that the letters can stand for *any* number. The notation is not meaningful to all students, but the entire group understands that the generalization it represents applies to all whole numbers, no matter how large.

Adding 1 to a Factor

Next Ms. Kaye asks her class to consider what happens when 1 is added to a factor in a multiplication expression. How does the product change? In posing the question involving multiplication immediately after the one involving addition, she focuses the attention of her students on the differences between the two operations.

As she did with addition, Ms. Kaye begins by presenting a set of equations to the class.

7 x 5 = 35	7 x 5 = 35
7 x 6 = 42	8 x 5 = 40
9 x 4 = 36	9 x 4 = 36
9 x 5 = 45	10 x 4 = 40

Students work individually to notice the regularity and articulate a claim, writing in a response to the following prompt: "In a multiplication problem, if you increase one of the factors by 1, I think this will happen to the product: _____ ." Ms. Kaye reviews their writing, seeing responses ranging from a description of a particular case (how the product of 9×4 is different from that of 9×5) to a statement of a general claim ("the product will go up by the number that you don't increase by 1").

The following day begins with a brief discussion of a chart of many of the students' statements. Then they work on the following task: Starting with either $7 \times 5 = 35$ or $9 \times 4 = 36$, write a story, draw a picture, or make an array for the equation. Then change the representation just enough to match $7 \times 6 = 42$ and $8 \times 5 = 40$ or $9 \times 5 = 45$ and $10 \times 4 = 40$. Finally, write what happens when one of the factors increases by 1.

Ms. Kaye begins the class discussion with Frannie's story context.

....

There are 7 jewelry boxes and each box has 5 pieces of jewelry. There are 35 pieces of jewelry altogether.

Ms. Kaye: Is this story about multiplication? How do you know?

Hannah: Because there's some amount of boxes, and some amount of things in the boxes. And how many things are in that many boxes.

Ms. Kaye: Does that sound like multiplication to you?

Class: Yes!

Ms. Kaye: Anything anybody wants to add to make absolutely sure it sounds like multiplication?

Helen: Instead of boxes it could be groups. So there are 7 groups of 5 pieces.

Ms. Kaye: Is it important that each box has 5 pieces?

Class: Yes.

Ms. Kaye: What if some boxes had 3 and some boxes had 4 and some boxes had 1?

Jonah: It wouldn't be multiplication.

Ms. Kaye: How can you change the story to make it about 8 times 5?

Clarissa: Instead of 7 boxes, it would be 8 boxes.

Ms. Kaye: What got increased?

Sierra: The first number.

Paula: Boxes.

> *7 boxes that each contain 5 pieces of jewelry corresponds to $7 \times 5 = 35$. As discussion continues, students explain that increasing the first factor by 1 corresponds to adding 1 more box, increasing the total number of pieces of jewelry by the number of pieces in 1 box: $8 \times 5 = 40$. When the second number increases by 1, 1 piece of jewelry is added to each box, increasing the total number of pieces of jewelry by the number of boxes: $7 \times 6 = 42$.*
>
> *Then Ms. Kaye asks the class to think in more general terms.*

Ms. Kaye: I want to ask the group something. Is the jewelry and box situation only going to work when you have 7 boxes and 5 pieces of jewelry in there?

Students: No.

Manuel: It can work with 8 times 5.

Nora: It can work with 70 times 5.

Matt: It can work with any number.

Ms. Kaye: Can you resay the story?

Carl: There is any number of boxes of jewelry. Each box has any number of pieces of jewelry.

> *He is unable to finish. But Clarissa, remembering the notation the class used to formulate the generalization on addition, suggests working with* a times b.

Ms. Kaye: There's *a* boxes of jewelry; each box has *b* pieces of jewelry; and so the product is *c*, the number of jewelry pieces?

After the class agrees that a × b = c represents the context, Ms. Kaye points to Frannie's picture of 8 boxes, each with 5 pieces of jewelry.

Ms. Kaye: So what would this one be?

Helen: It would be *a* plus 1 times *b* pieces of jewelry equals *c* plus *b*.

The class works through the statements, producing the following equations:

$$a \times b = c$$

$$(a + 1) \times b = c + b$$

$$a \times (b + 1) = c + a$$

Addison and Ms. Kaye offer concluding statements:

Addison: If you increase the first number by 1, you increase the answer by the second number. Like if you increase *a* by 1, you increase the product by *b*. If you increase *b* by 1, you increase the answer by *a*.

Ms. Kaye: I love this context! Because you can have any number of jewelry boxes, each one with a certain number of jewels in it. And the product is going to be that multiplication. And if you increase the number of boxes, you get an increase by the number in each box. If you increase by 1 jewel, the increase is the number of boxes because each box gets 1 jewel.

Working with Frannie's context helps the students come to a clear articulation of the claim. The context also provides a representation-based proof satisfying all three criteria:

1. *The meaning of the operations involved in the claim is represented in the story context.* The multiplication is represented by some number of jewelry boxes, each containing a given number of pieces of jewelry. The product is the total number of pieces. Addition is represented by joining, with either an additional box joined to the group of original boxes or an additional piece of jewelry placed in each box.

2. *The representation can accommodate a class of instances.* There can be any whole number of boxes, each with any whole number of pieces of jewelry.

3. *The conclusion of the claim follows from the structure of the representation; that is, the representation shows why the statement must be true.* The students explain that adding 1 to the first factor means 1 more box, therefore increasing the

product by the number of pieces in a box; that is, increasing the product by the second factor. Adding 1 to the second factor increases the number of pieces in each box by 1, increasing the total number of jewels by the number of boxes, which is the first factor.

Although the class has proved the claim according to these criteria, Ms. Kaye recognizes that her students still need to think through and internalize these ideas. The lesson continues with students examining the other pictures, arrays, and story contexts they created.

In closing, Ms. Kaye asks the class to compare their generalization for adding 1 to an addend in an addition expression with their generalization for adding 1 to a factor in a multiplication expression.

Ms. Kaye: [*The generalizations*] **help us notice how multiplication is really different from addition. If one of the parts is increased by 1 in addition, the result is what? 1 more. If one of the parts is increased by 1 in multiplication, then it increases by the other part.**

Addison: In addition, both of the numbers behave the same. But in multiplication, each has a little bit of a different role.

Frannie: One keeps track of this one thing; the other keeps track of this other thing.

By justifying these claims, the students learn to think in terms of *all whole numbers*, and articulate and clarify distinctions among the operations.

FIFTH GRADERS CONSIDER INTEGERS AND RATIONAL NUMBERS

As students progress through school, they repeatedly encounter new kinds of numbers. Children first learn about counting numbers starting at 1, and then consider 0. In later elementary grades, they work with fractions, decimals, and negative numbers.

When students study a generalization, they apply it to the number domains with which they are familiar. Many of their representations require whole numbers to make sense. For example, the story about boxes and pieces of jewelry requires whole numbers of boxes and pieces of jewelry. Before investigating whether a generalization is true for negative numbers, fractions, or decimals, students must first be familiar with representations that can accommodate such numbers.

In the following episodes, students use number lines to help them think about negative numbers and rectangles to think about fractions.

Extending a Generalization to Integers[3]

Consider an episode from Marlena Diaz's fifth-grade classroom. Students are examining subtraction expressions equal to 50. Like Isabel Hazelton's second graders, they recognize that if the two numbers of a subtraction expression are changed by the same amount, the difference remains the same. Alex demonstrates this on a number line.

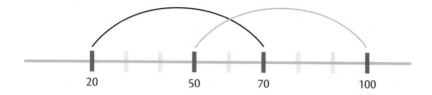

Alex represents subtraction as the distance from one number to another: 70 − 20 is the distance from 20 to 70, or the amount you add to 20 to get to 70. Alex demonstrates that sliding both the 20 and the 70 thirty steps to the right to 50 and 100 leaves the distance the same. Adding 30 to both numbers leaves the result unchanged: 70 − 20 = 100 − 50.

With this idea in mind, the class lists the following:

$$100 - 50$$

$$90 - 40$$

$$80 - 30$$

$$70 - 20$$

$$60 - 10$$

$$50 - 0$$

They start with 100 − 50. To find each equivalent expression, they subtract 10 from each number in the previous expression.

The question arises whether the sequence could continue. Some students argue that once you reach 0, you're done. But others argue that you could consider negative numbers, for example, 40 − −10.

To think about subtraction of integers, students must expand their images of the operations. They cannot rely on contexts such as taking away baseball cards, because there is no meaning for −10 cards. Alex uses the number line to make sense of 40 − −10.

---

3   The set of integers consists of the set of counting numbers (1, 2, 3, 4, . . .), their additive inverses (−1, −2, −3, −4, . . .), and 0.

Alex: It is like adding 10, because if you look on the number line, you would have to jump 50 to get from negative 10 to 40. It is the same as we did with 100 and 50 and 70 and 20.

Ms. Diaz: So, Alex, how do you know that 40 minus negative 10 will give you 50?

Alex: Because you have to add 50 to negative 10 to get 40.

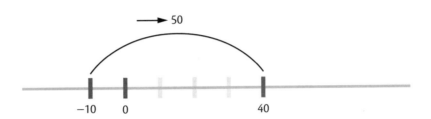

To represent $100 - 50$ and $70 - 20$, Alex uses the distance between the two numbers on the number line. Because this interpretation of subtraction extends to points to the left of 0, Alex has shown that $40 - {}^-10$ must also equal 50.

Whenever students consider a new set of numbers, they need to reconsider many of the generalizations they have made. For example, they may have concluded that subtraction always results in a difference smaller than or equal to the minuend, capturing this idea with the phrase "Subtraction makes things smaller." They may also have concluded that changing both numbers in a subtraction problem by the same amount leaves the difference the same. Both of these statements are true for all whole numbers. However, in the realm of integers, the second statement is true, but the first is not.

Some of Alex's classmates are surprised that $40 - {}^-10$ could equal 50; how can you subtract from 40 and get a result that is larger than 40? Over time, with the help of a number line and other representations, these students will sort out how the operations of addition and subtraction work with negative numbers. These ideas need not be investigated fully in the elementary grades, but observations like Alex's prepare students' minds for future investigations. As students move into the realms of integers and rational numbers, they will continually reexamine their generalizations about the operations to make sure that they still apply.

Extending a Generalization to Rational Numbers[4]

Later in the year, the same class is working on a different generalization. In their language, "If you do 'something' to one of the factors (multiply), you have to do the

---

4   The set of rational numbers consists of those numbers that can be represented as $\frac{a}{b}$, where a and b are integers and $b \neq 0$. Fractions and decimals are different ways to notate rational numbers.

opposite 'something' to the other factor (divide) if you want to have the same product you had before you did the two 'somethings.'" In other words, given a multiplication expression, if one factor is multiplied by some amount and the other factor is divided by that same amount, the product stays the same.

The class uses arrays of squares to represent this generalization. For example, for $18 \times 4 = 6 \times 12$, 18 can be divided by 3 and 4 multiplied by 3 to get 6×12. The arrays below represent the equivalence of the two expressions.

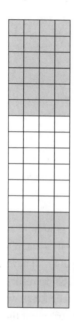
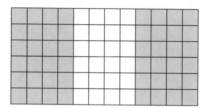

The 18×4 array is divided into three 6×4 sections, which are then rearranged to create a 6×12 array. The students comment that this can be done for any array.

....

David: Basically all you are doing is breaking it apart and putting it back together in a different way.

Keila: And you can keep doing that with all the factors but don't add any more squares.

....

The students are saying that you can divide the vertical length by any of its factors to make the smaller arrays, and then rearrange them to create the new array. Because the action doesn't involve adding or removing any squares, the two arrays are composed of the same number of square units. That is, the products of the two expressions are the same.

Ms. Diaz's next question takes the students out of the realm of whole numbers.

What if we used a number that isn't one of the factors? Could we still change the rectangle?

Keila's insistence that the divisor be a factor of the original (whole) number assures that the quotient will also be a whole number. By removing that restriction, Ms. Diaz opens up the possibility of a fractional quotient.

....

David: You could but you would have to cut some of the squares.

Katherine: The squares can show us some numbers, but it is harder to show others. If you use an odd number and divide it by 2, you would have to get a decimal.

Ms. Diaz: So what about this representation are you thinking is hard to show?

Katherine: If you had like a 10 by ½. How could you show ½?

Salena: You would have to cut 1 square like David said.

....

Students in Ms. Diaz's class *imagine* fractional squares to extend their generalization to include fractions. For example, these diagrams represent $3 \times 5 = 6 \times 2.5$.

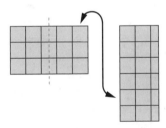

As Salena and David said, one column of squares must be cut in half to create a rectangular arrangement that shows 6 by 2.5.

A more flexible representation for multiplication is the area of a rectangle. This representation has a subtle difference from an array. An array of squares implies whole-number values (number of rows × number of items in a row = number of objects in the array), and a rectangle allows dimensions of any positive number (length of one dimension × length of second dimension = area of rectangle). Trish and Emily's poster, with which we began this chapter, is such an area representation. It shows that for *any* positive values, T and E, $T \times E = \frac{1}{2}T \times 2E$. T and E can be fractions or decimal numbers.

Can Trish and Emily's representation be adapted to extend their generalization further to show that $T \times E = (T \div n) \times (E \times n)$? And for what values of n is this true?

IN CONCLUSION . . .

In this chapter, we have examined students as they considered general claims about the behavior of operations and addressed whether these claims were true for all numbers. By creating representations for their generalizations, students were able to come to clearer articulations of their claims. In some cases, their representations also helped them develop a proof or argument for their claim.

Many first graders consider only relatively small whole numbers when they reason about how the operations behave. By third grade, students begin to realize that positive whole numbers extend infinitely and extend their claims to take this into account. By fifth grade, as students become more familiar with integers and rational numbers, claims that were formulated for whole numbers must be reconsidered. Does dividing one factor by 2 and multiplying the other factor by 2 result in equivalent multiplication expressions even when numbers in the original or resulting expression are fractions or decimals?

To investigate such questions, students must consider which representations can accommodate fractions, decimals, or negative numbers and which cannot. For example, an array consisting of identical, intact squares cannot represent multiplication involving fractional factors, but a rectangle can. The number line students have used to represent subtraction involving positive numbers can be extended to serve as a model for subtraction involving negative numbers.

As students move beyond the elementary grades, they will encounter still other kinds of numbers. They will discover that the number line contains irrational numbers, which are not whole numbers, integers, or rational numbers. Later, they will learn that there are numbers, called *imaginary numbers*, not even contained on the number line.

Proving that a claim applies to the infinite set of whole numbers is an enormous achievement for elementary students. Such claims should be acknowledged even if they are not true for negative numbers or fractions (for example, a product is greater than its factors, unless the factors include 0 or 1). However, as students move into a new number domain, teachers must ensure that students carefully rethink their generalizations, acknowledging the reasonableness of the generalizations formulated within one domain while helping students make sense of the behavior of the operations in the extended domain. ■

DEVELOPING MATHEMATICAL ARGUMENTS: WHAT IS THE DOMAIN?

1. In Chapter 8, students examine what happens to their thinking when the set of numbers they are accustomed to considering expands. For the youngest students this means considering "very" large numbers; for older students it means moving from positive whole numbers to rational numbers or to negative integers. Provide an example of this kind of thinking from your own grade level: where does this idea of expanding the meaning of number happen for your students?

2. Examine the teacher-student interaction in the excerpt about Ms. Callendar's class. How do the specific questions she asks both support and challenge her students?

3. In the first part of Ms. Kaye's lesson on addition, the third graders make claims about "all whole numbers." Two different posters are detailed. Explain what idea each poster illustrates. What does each representation indicate about the students' understanding?

4. Examine the teacher-student interaction in the lesson from Ms. Kaye's class on adding 1 to a factor. What mathematical ideas is this class working on? How do the specific questions Ms. Kaye asks both support and challenge her students?

5. What new mathematical ideas are Ms. Diaz's class encountering in the lesson "Extending a Generalization to Integers"? What new ideas do these students encounter in the lesson "Extending a Generalization to Rational Numbers"? In what ways does Ms. Diaz draw her students' attention to these issues?

9

Looking Ahead to the Middle Grades

Throughout this book, we have examined the potential for elementary students to engage in algebraic thinking and the benefits they gain from doing so. Now, we look ahead at how understanding the behavior of the operations can benefit middle school mathematics students and help them overcome some of the difficulties they commonly encounter.

WHAT'S HARD ABOUT MIDDLE SCHOOL CONTENT

Middle school math teachers find that some students consistently make the same errors. For example, some students repeatedly and incorrectly write equations like these:[1]

$$(a + b)^2 = a^2 + b^2$$

$$2(xy) = (2x)(2y)$$

---

1 In algebraic notation, the symbol "×," indicating multiplication, is not used. Frequently, "·" is used instead of "×." That is, $a \cdot b$ means $a \times b$. When there is no symbol between variables or expressions, multiplication is understood: xy means $x \times y$, and $n(a + b)$ means $n \times (a + b)$. Both of these notations are used in this chapter.

Students persist in these errors even after being corrected. When asked why they believe these equations are true, students often refer to other situations that they take to be similar, such as $2(a + b) = 2a + 2b$. They think that they should "distribute the 2" in the same way. The error arises because the students consider a superficial pattern of symbols rather than think about the operations the symbols represent. In this case, they may be thinking of the distributive property of multiplication over addition, which is correctly represented as $(a + b)n = an + bn$ or as $n(a + b) = na + nb$ (in the case of $n = 2$, $2(a + b) = 2a + 2b$).

Bill Lancaster is a middle school teacher who works individually with students. A mathematician who started teaching late in life, he tries to understand the thinking of students who come to him with various difficulties. He writes:

> *I used to think that the fundamental difficulty had to do with the introduction of variables, and with expressions and formulas now used for reasoning about arithmetic rather than doing arithmetic. In elementary school $4 + 5 = \_\_$ has a clear interpretation (similar to what a calculator makes of these marks): "take the number 4 and take the number 5 and add them now, and what matters is the number that results, the answer." In middle school, students see $x + 5 = y$ and yet there is no obvious adding to be done, and it isn't clear what an answer would look like. Though "+" and "=" look like the same symbols they have always used, they no longer trigger actions the same way.*

> *More recently, I've come to think that an even more fundamental difficulty has to do with the understanding of multiplication as distinct from addition. The conclusion I'm coming to is that the students who have the deepest trouble with middle school mathematics are those without a clear and rich set of models for what multiplication is and how it is different from addition. In the absence of such models, the students tend to rely increasingly on memorizing rules and how-tos, and their grasp is tentative and fragile. They have given up trying to make sense of what they are doing, and instead rely on their quite well-honed skills of guessing what the teacher wants. To my surprise, this includes many of the students who have decent grades and who can get by quite well with symbolic manipulation of formulas that may hold very little meaning for them.*

Mr. Lancaster illustrates this issue by describing his work with Joy, an eighth grader having difficulty with her assignments. Joy's class has been working with rectangular representations of multiplicative expressions like the one for $14 \cdot 12$ shown on the following page. The factors correspond to the lengths of the sides of the rectangle and are represented as $10 + 4$ and $10 + 2$. The area of the rectangle can be seen as the product of the lengths of the two sides: $14 \cdot 12 = (10 + 4)(10 + 2)$. It can also be seen as the sum of the areas of the four smaller rectangles: $100 + 40 + 20 + 8$. Thus, this representation shows $14 \cdot 12 = (10 + 4)(10 + 2) = 100 + 40 + 20 + 8$.

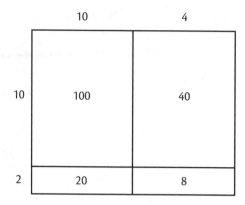

Joy's teacher has been using similar diagrams to represent multiplying binomials,[2] such as $(x + 4)(x + 2)$. When Mr. Lancaster presents Joy with the figure on the left, she knows exactly how to produce the figure on the right. She fills in the boxes on the right and writes the sum: $x^2 + 4x + 2x + 8$. Joy calls the sum the "expanded form" (this form shows all four subproducts). She is also supposed to produce the factored form (the form showing the expressions being multiplied), but here she has difficulty. She tries $(x \cdot x) + (2 \cdot 4)$, but this doesn't look right to her, so she tries $(4x)(2x)$, which is also incorrect.

Joy's ability to fill out the picture on the right *seems* to imply a good understanding of multiplication of binomials. However, it turns out that she is only copying a procedure she watched her teacher do. For the representation to be meaningful, a student must grasp that the lengths of the sides of the large rectangle are obtained by *adding* the lengths of the segments to get $x + 4$ and $x + 2$. The area, which represents the product of the binomials, is obtained by *multiplying* the lengths of the sides, giving

2 A binomial is an expression with two addends (terms), each of which is a variable, a constant, or a product of variables and/or constants. For example, $x + 4$, $a^2 + b^2$, and $7n^2 + 5n$ are binomials, whereas $x + y + 3xy^2$ is not (it's a *trinomial*).

$(x + 4)(x + 2)$. Because the area of the large rectangle is equal to the sum of the four smaller rectangles, $(x + 4)(x + 2) = x^2 + 4x + 2x + 8$.

At first glance, Joy's problem might seem to arise from her misunderstanding of variables. But her attempts to write the multiplication expressions represented in the diagram as $(x \cdot x) + (2 \cdot 4)$ and $(4x)(2x)$ argue that she has an underlying problem in visualizing the operations. She is not clear on when to multiply and when to add, and she doesn't connect these operations to the sides and areas of the rectangles. Joy does not understand that the lengths of the sides can be represented as $(x + 4)$ and $(x + 2)$ and that the area is the product of those lengths, $(x + 4)(x + 2)$.

Joe is another of Mr. Lancaster's eighth graders having trouble with the distributive property. For Joe, Mr. Lancaster draws a series of rectangles divided into two parts.

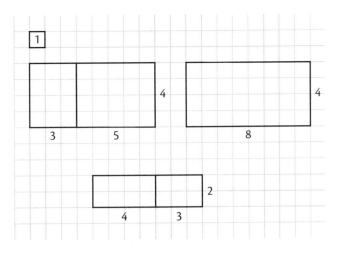

Mr. Lancaster describes what happens:

> I suggested to Joe that we were looking at tiles, and rooms, and houses. The top picture was a single tile, and below was a house split into two rooms. I asked Joe how many tiles were needed for each room. He counted each one out: 12 for the left room, and 20 for the right room. I drew the same house on the right, but didn't show the two rooms. I asked how many tiles it would take to cover the whole house. Joe started counting, but then switched to looking at each of the sides, 4 and 8, and he said "32." I asked how he had come to that answer so quickly, and he said: "I did 4 times 8." I then asked what the total number of tiles was that was needed for the house on the left, and he added 12 and 20, getting 32. I asked Joe what he noticed. He said: "I'm getting the same as the other house." I asked how come. He offered that it was really the same house, just looking at the whole house in one case, and the separate rooms in the other. I wrote down:

$$3 \cdot 4 + 5 \cdot 4 = 8 \cdot 4$$

I took Joe through the same exercise with the bottom house, and he correctly got the left room as 4 · 2 and the right room as 3 · 2. The total house? He said: "4 times 2 equals 8, and 3 times 2 equals 6, so 8 plus 6 equals 14." I asked how he would find the total number of tiles needed if he couldn't go inside, but could only look at the outside of the house. He came up with 7 · 2, also 14. I wrote down:

$$4 \cdot 2 + 3 \cdot 2 = 7 \cdot 2$$

I asked if he noticed a pattern in the two statements I'd written down. "Both have a 3 in it, and both have a 4 in it," he ventured.

Joe solves each problem, but he seems not to notice how multiplication and addition work together—that there is a connection between 4 · 2, 3 · 2, and 7 · 2. When asked what he notices, Joe mentions specific numbers rather than relationships among operations.

Joy and Joe are two of the many students who are trying to learn algebra without making meaning for the symbols. What can happen in the elementary grades that would better prepare students like Joy and Joe?

Careful analysis of their difficulties indicate some answers to this question. For Joy, one specific problem is an incomplete understanding of the rectangular representation for binomial multiplication. She does not seem to realize that the area of the large rectangle can be obtained both by multiplying the lengths of the sides and by adding the areas of the four smaller rectangles, and that because the two expressions represent the same thing, they can be written as two sides of an equation. Activities to develop fluency with arrays and rectangular representations (such as those performed by Marlena Diaz's students in Chapter 8) would support students like Joy.

A more general difficulty is evident as Joy tries several ways to factor the expression $x^2 + 4x + 2x + 8$. She mixes up addition and multiplication without consideration of how these different operations behave. She would benefit from participating in discussions about how addition is different from multiplication.

Joe is able to use an array representation, but he does not attempt to make generalizations about the operations. He sees mathematics as solving specific problems and is satisfied to solve each of the problems Mr. Lancaster gives him. When asked if he notices anything about a set of examples, Joe seems not to understand the question.

Joe may have been quite successful in mathematics up until now, because his task has been to compute answers accurately and efficiently. However, because he has never before had to consider generalizations about the behavior of the operations, he is now at a loss in algebra, where he must understand and apply the distributive property.

We now focus on classrooms where middle school teachers emphasize reasoning about the behavior of the operations, building on the approaches used in elementary grades as described in Chapters 1 through 8.

UNDERSTANDING WHOLE-NUMBER MULTIPLICATION AND DIVISION AS A SUPPORT FOR UNDERSTANDING FRACTIONS

Middle school students are generally assumed to be competent at whole-number calculations, so attention turns to working with fractions and integers. Many students consider this effort to be completely separate from earlier studies. They believe fractions and integers require entirely new sets of procedures. Teachers can help their students to revisit their knowledge of the behaviors of operations, and apply this knowledge to these new number domains.

In Sandy O'Grady's sixth-grade class, students are working with problems requiring them to combine or subtract fractions with different denominators. One problem involves adding 2⅝ ounces of nutmeg and 4¼ ounces of cinnamon. Edward successfully solves the problem by adding the whole number and fractional amounts separately to end up with 6⅞ ounces of spice.

Ms. O'Grady regularly encourages students who feel they have mastered one method to try to find a different method. Edward notices a student at his table calculating by changing all the mixed numbers to improper fractions. He wants to try this. After several minutes, he raises his hand and says, "Ms. O'Grady, I cannot remember how to change 2⅝ so it is not a mixed number. Do I divide the 2 by 8 or do I multiply?"

Rather than answering directly, Ms. O'Grady asks him to select a fraction model for 2⅝, and he chooses a set of "fraction circles" from a nearby shelf.

⋯⋯⋯⋯⋯⋯⋯⋯⋯⋯⋯⋯⋯⋯⋯⋯⋯⋯⋯⋯⋯⋯

Ms. O'Grady: You can use these fraction-circle pieces or draw them in your journal. Before you get started, let me ask you one more question. What do multiplication and division mean?

Edward: Multiplication is about groups of equal groups. Division can be breaking into equal groups or finding how many fit in.

Ms. O'Grady: I think that with your circle models and with what you know about the meaning of multiplication and division, you can sort out what to do with this and why. I want you to change 2 and ⅝ to an improper fraction and ¹⁷⁄₃ to a mixed number. Be prepared to explain to me how to do this and why it works.

Ms. O'Grady leaves for a few minutes, then returns to look at Edward's representation and hear his thinking.

Edward: I get it now. To add the 2 whole circles to the ⅝ of a circle *[points at his drawings]*, you have to change the whole circles into eighths so they have the same-size pieces. That's 2 groups of 8 or 2 times 8. So sixteen-eighths and five-eighths is twenty-one-eighths. I think I was confused because there is both division and multiplication *[points to the circles that he has divided into eighths]*.

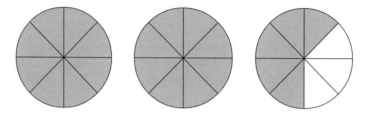

When I divide the whole circles into eighths, I get groups of 8 eighths so it is multiplication. With the other problem *[¹⁷⁄₃]*, I was fitting thirds together to make a whole. This is "How many fits in?" so it's division.

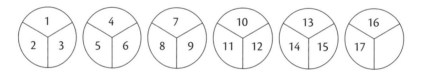

....

Ms. O'Grady then gives Edward two more numbers and he is able to explain how to convert them.

When Edward originally asked how to change a mixed number into an improper fraction, he may have expected to be told a procedure. But once Ms. O'Grady prompts him to answer the question for himself, Edward knows how to proceed. He knows how to represent 2⅝, and he knows that his goal is to represent the quantity in terms of some number of eighths. His representation activates his understanding that multiplication involves finding the quantity contained in a set of equal groups, and he sees that he needs to *multiply* the number of whole circles by 8. This makes 16 eighths in 2 wholes, which he adds to 5 to get ²¹⁄₈. He uses a similar representation to convert ¹⁷⁄₃ to a mixed number. Because each circle contains 3 thirds, he *divides* 17 by 3 to find the number of groups of size 3. There are 5 whole groups and another ⅔ of a group, so he concludes that ¹⁷⁄₃ = 5⅔.

As Edward engages in this process, he is not simply trying to solve two specific problems involving 2⅝ and ¹⁷⁄₃. Rather, he is working with these numbers to develop a generalized procedure. He can picture *any* mixed number as a series of wholes divided into fractional parts, which he can then convert to an improper fraction. He can use a similar image to group any improper fraction into wholes to determine an equivalent mixed number. To develop such general procedures, it is not sufficient that Edward simply know multiplication and division *calculations*. He must also understand the *behavior* of the operations.

Edward's image of whole-number multiplication and division involves equal groups. It allows him to reason about converting mixed numbers to improper fractions and vice versa. However, as students encounter multiplication and division of fractions, some of their representations may no longer work. For example, how can a representation of multiplication as equal groupings be used to interpret ¼ · ½? This expression contains *no whole groups*. On the other hand, consider a rectangle such as the one below:

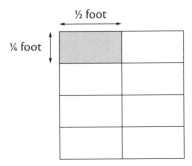

A rectangle whose sides are ½ foot and ¼ foot has an area equal to ⅛ square foot.

Students fluent with *multiple* representations of operations can learn to select the representation best suited for each context. Fraction circles or number lines may work well for reasoning about addition and subtraction with fractions, for example, and rectangular representations for multiplication and division.

EXTENDING CONTEXTS TO MAKE SENSE OF INTEGERS

Negative numbers are rarely used in everyday life. Quantities we could refer to with negative numbers are usually described in other terms: instead of talking about having −$5, we say we have a debt of $5; instead of talking about −4°, we say 4 degrees below zero. Many students find using contexts to help them think through operations with integers challenging.

In Liam Hamilton's seventh-grade class, students have become familiar with several different models for working with integers: a horizontal number line that includes numbers to the left of 0, different-colored chips representing dollars in the bank and dollars owed, and a hot air balloon rising and descending. Students use these models to represent operations with the integers.

Mr. Hamilton asks his class to represent $3 \cdot -4$ with one of the models. Mr. Hamilton moves from group to group, questioning students about their thinking. He stops at Ken, Mel, and Paige's table to discuss their model. They have laid out 3 black chips, 4 red chips, and 12 red chips.

Mr. Hamilton: Ken, please explain this picture to me.

Ken: The 3 is positive so that would be 3 black chips and the 4 is negative and so that would be 4 red chips. When you multiply these you get negative 12, so we have 12 red chips.

Mel: It is 12 red chips because we know a positive times a negative is a negative.

Mr. Hamilton: How do you know that?

Mel: It just is.

Mr. Hamilton: That sounds like math magic to me. What happens when I put these chips together?

Paige: You end up with 1 red chip or $1 that you owe because 3 red chips with the 3 black chips equal 0.

Mr. Hamilton: So how does this all of a sudden become negative 12? [*The team is quiet.*] **I want you to review again what multiplication means as a team and then see if you can come up with another way to use the chips to represent the problem.**

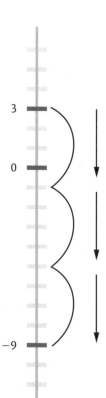

This group already knows that $3 \cdot -4$ should equal -12, and their model includes these numbers. However, the model doesn't illustrate the meaning of multiplication. The students do not yet understand why $3 \cdot -4 = -12$.

Another group struggles with the hot air balloon model, which they have represented on a vertical number line. Their hot air balloon starts at positive 3 to represent the 3 in the multiplication problem. Unlike the previous group, they have a sense there should be 3 groups of something. They have drawn 3 arrows showing 3 consecutive jumps of -4 down their number line. The last arrow ends at -9.

Ami: I don't get it. The balloon is at negative 9, but it should be negative 12. The answer is negative 12.

Mr. Hamilton: That is a puzzle. Before you go any further, I want you as a team to discuss two questions. First, is there another way to see 12 in your diagram? Second, I see 3 as the starting place for your balloon, but I also see 3 arrows. Which of these is the 3 in 3 times negative 4?

⋯⋯⋯⋯⋯⋯⋯⋯⋯⋯⋯⋯⋯⋯⋯⋯⋯⋯⋯⋯⋯⋯

In response to his students' confusion, Mr. Hamilton asks them to think about the meaning of multiplication and how it applies in their diagram. What is the role of 3 in the expression $3 \cdot -4$? Will they see that 3 jumps of -4 could show the balloon's descent of 12 feet (a change in the balloon's height of -12)?

After about forty minutes, all groups are ready to present their work. Mr. Hamilton begins the discussion with the two groups described above because he wants all students to grapple with the questions these groups found difficult. How can one understand the meaning of multiplication in a way that explains the role of 3 in the problem? Can the 3 be represented as a physical number of chips or a position on the number line? Mr. Hamilton pushes his students' understanding of multiplication deeper so they can relate it to negative numbers.

After some initial discussion, a third group presents a different hot air balloon model. Theirs starts at 0, making the -12 both the change of the balloon's elevation and its final position on the number line. Ami's group acknowledges that this representation makes more sense than theirs.

After the third group's presentation, there is just enough time for Paige to explain how her group resolved their confusion.

We thought more about what multiplication means and decided to start with a story and then try to model the story with chips. In multiplication, one of the numbers is the number of groups. We thought of owing 3 different people $4. A debt of $4 is negative 4. So we owe a total of $12. In our poster, we have 3 groups of 4 red chips. This is a total of 12 red chips or negative 12.

Students in this class can represent 3 and –4 and already know that the product is –12. Still, it is a challenge for them to connect their interpretations of negative numbers with the meaning of multiplying 3 and –4. As a class, they are able to devise two contexts and associated representations that do this: a hot air balloon that descends 4 feet 3 times, and a picture of 3 groups of 4 red chips that corresponds to owing $4 to each of 3 people. These contexts build on and extend representations for multiplication of whole numbers developed in the elementary grades.

CREATING IMAGES FOR ALGEBRAIC EXPRESSIONS

Learning to work with variables is a major component of middle school mathematics. Students can merely learn a set of rules for manipulating symbols, or they can develop meaning for the symbols in order to reason about these manipulations.

Students in Cynthia McLeod's seventh-grade class are working on the distributive property of multiplication over addition with expressions involving variables. They have previously demonstrated the distributive property for specific numbers. For 4 · 12, one group of students made up this story: 4 basketball teams play in a tournament. Each team has 10 players and 2 coaches. You can determine the total number of people in two ways:

1. Multiply 4 (the number of teams) times 12 (10 players plus 2 coaches) to get 48.

2. Multiply 4 times 10 to get 40, the total number of players; multiply 4 times 2 to get 8, the total number of coaches; add 40 and 8 to get 48.

Because both methods—4 · 12 and (4 · 10) + (4 · 2)—result in the same product, the two expressions must be equal. A rectangular representation would look like:

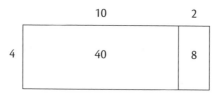

Again, because the area of the rectangle can be seen both as the product of the sides, 4 · 12, and as the sum of the areas of the smaller two rectangles, (4 · 10) + (4 · 2), the two expressions must be equal.

Building on this review of the distributive property with whole numbers, Ms. McLeod asks students to devise representations for $3(x + 4)$. After about twenty minutes, she begins a whole-class discussion.

....

Ms. McLeod: We will start the whole-group discussion by having Ann's group and Sean's group share their thinking. As they do, I want you to be looking for connections you see between their representations.

Ann: We started with a story. We are a company that makes special-order hammocks designed to fit the person ordering the hammock. We think an ideal-size hammock is 4 feet longer than the height of the person ordering. So each hammock needs to be the height of the person plus 4 feet longer. Heights are different for different people so that is x. We have a special price if you order 3. If someone orders 3 hammocks for a person who is x feet tall, that uses $3(x + 4)$ feet of material. We used tiles to create a hammock. [*Ann points to her group's poster.*] One long tile stands for *x* and each little square tile is 1. If you put 3 of our tile hammocks together, you end up with 3*x*s and 3 groups of 4 units. You get 3*x* plus 12.

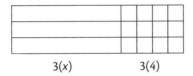

3(*x*)   3(4)

Sean: Our team thought about what multiplication means. 3 times $(x + 4)$ is 3 groups of $(x + 4)$. If *x* was 10, then this would be $14 + 14 + 14$. So 3 times $(x + 4)$ equals $(x + 4) + (x + 4) + (x + 4)$.

Ms. McLeod: OK, I want each group to take the next four minutes to talk about the connections you see between these two representations. Are they the same? What do they do to help you make meaning for the expression $3(x + 4)$?

These students are expected to make connections among different algebraic expressions, story contexts, and diagrams, just as elementary students make connections among arithmetic expressions, story contexts, and diagrams. Because each representation may highlight different aspects of the mathematics, looking across representations offers a richer set of connections and thus deeper understanding. The symbols and procedures, too often considered meaningless, are imbued with meaning.

CREATING IMAGES FOR EQUIVALENT EQUATIONS

Solving equations is a major topic in beginning algebra courses. Given an equation such as $3x + 7 = 19$, solving means finding the value of *x* that makes the equation true. Standard procedure is to create a series of equivalent equations ending with an equation giving the value of *x*. For example:

$$3x + 7 = 19$$

$$3x = 12$$

$$x = 4$$

These three equations are equivalent—any value of *x* that makes one equation true also makes the other equations true. Subtracting 7 from both sides of $3x + 7 = 19$ yields $3x = 12$. Dividing both sides of $3x = 12$ by 3 results in the equivalent equation $x = 4$. When the value of *x* is 4, all three equations are true. The *solution* of $3x + 7 = 19$ is 4.

For many students, these rules for finding x are mysterious. Even when they learn the procedures and can perform them correctly and efficiently, they cannot relate them to any other form of representation or context.

Jaden Singer introduces a variety of representations to help his pre-algebra students bring meaning to the procedures they are learning. Recently, his class has been using balance scales to represent the process of solving equations. He feels this model will help students keep track of the meaning of equality while using inversely related operations to solve equations. A "mystery bag"—which contains an unknown number of blocks—represents the variable.

To begin the series of lessons, Mr. Singer asks his students to describe how a balance scale works. It is important they understand that if a quantity is added or removed from one side of the scale, the same quantity must be added or removed from the other side to keep the scale in balance.

Mr. Singer presents this picture for students to consider.

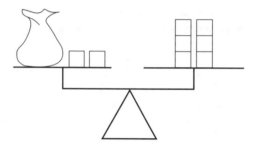

Some students suggest that the mystery bag contains 4 cubes. Mr. Singer presses for an explanation: "How could you convince someone that doesn't believe you that the mystery bag contains 4 cubes?"

Aleesha says, "Because if the bag contains 4 cubes and there are already 2 other cubes on that side of the balance, then those 6 cubes are the same amount as the 6 cubes on the other side, and the scale will be in balance."

Mr. Singer waits patiently for students to acknowledge Aleesha's explanation and to see if another explanation surfaces. Carlos raises his hand and tentatively offers: "I thought about removing 2 cubes from each side of the scale. Since I removed the same amount, the scale should still be in balance. But now I have just the mystery bag on one side and 4 cubes on the other." Mr. Singer points out the differences between Aleesha's "getting the same amount on each side" strategy and Carlos' strategy for isolating the mystery bag on one side of the scale.

Over the next two days, students use the balance scale to solve a series of problems. On the third day, Mr. Singer presents the following problem for students to represent with the balance scale model and then solve for x:

$$\frac{3}{4}x = 12$$

Travers and Marcus debate how to best draw three-fourths of a mystery bag. Travers wants to draw a smaller than normal bag "since ¾ is less than 1." Marcus is concerned with showing how much less. After pondering for a few moments he draws a mystery box instead of a mystery bag. Then he draws horizontal line segments across the box that divide it into 4 slices and shades 3 of the 4 parts. "It's like the shaded parts are filled with cubes, and the unshaded part isn't."

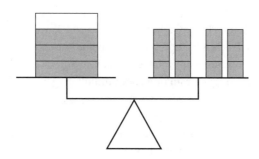

Travers accepts Marcus' representation, but the boys cannot decide what to do next. Their conversation makes it clear that they aren't sure what question they are trying to answer.

Mr. Singer: So, in the past when you have been working with mystery bag problems, what were you trying to figure out?

Marcus: How many cubes are in a bag. We changed the bag into a box, but we don't even have a full box of cubes.

Mr. Singer: Perhaps the question we need to answer is the same as before— find out how many cubes are in a *full* box—and we know that a box that is only three-fourths full contains 12 cubes.

Marcus: Oh, it's like x *is* something, and we want to find what x is.

Marcus' comment makes it clear that he sees something more to this work than mystery bags (or boxes) and scales. Until now, Marcus just manipulated symbols or shifted cubes to find the value of x that made the equation true or the scales balance. Now he suddenly finds new meaning. When the box is partially filled, x stands for the capacity of the box when full. Figuring out what x means in the context of the scale representation brings Marcus to a deeper and more precise understanding of solving equations.

To finish the problem, Marcus draws arrows connecting each cube on the right side of the balance to one of the 3 shaded slices in the box on the left. He seems to be trying to distribute the 12 cubes evenly among the 3 shaded sections. Travers points out that there are 4 sections of the box, and says that the cubes should be distributed evenly among all 4 sections. Marcus reminds him that only the shaded parts contain cubes.

Noticing that each shaded part corresponds to 4 cubes, the boys conclude that the unshaded part would also get 4 cubes, implying that a full box contains 16 cubes.

Mr. Singer calls the class together for Marcus and Travers to present their strategy. He then asks the class to represent Marcus and Travers' work symbolically. Mr. Singer asks if their actions are related to multiplying or dividing. Just before the period ends, Asada suggests thinking about multiplying both sides by ⅓. Mr. Singer ends by asking that the class consider Asada's suggestion in terms of Marcus and Travers' diagram.

This prealgebra class uses visual representations to make sense of the steps they employ to "solve for x." Their work demonstrates that the ability to connect the scale representation to algebraic symbols requires that students come to the task with an understanding of the actions of the operations.

REASONING FROM THE LAWS OF ARITHMETIC

Proof in higher grades does not rely on representations in the way that proof has been depicted in this book. Consider a question posed by Shane in Liam Hamilton's seventh-grade class after the session mentioned previously:

> If the problem is 3 times 4, then you can have 3 groups of 4, which is the same as 4 groups of 3. They both equal 12. How can that be with 3 times negative 4? How can you have negative 4 groups?

The class has been using the balloon context and the chip context to represent integer multiplication. One group represented $3 \cdot -4$ as 3 descents of 4 feet, and the other used 3 debts of $4 to represent the same problem. Shane is asking how either representation can be used to think about $-4 \cdot 3$. Does it make sense to ascend 3 feet -4 times? How can you owe -4 people $3? Does the expression $-4 \cdot 3$ even make sense?

Mr. Hamilton does challenge his class to come up with contexts to help answer Shane. However, there is another way to think about his questions. At a certain point, mathematicians *choose* to work with a set of rules to make the number system consistent. One might say to Shane that $-4 \cdot 3$ is equal to -12 *because we choose to maintain the commutative property of multiplication*. Because it has been determined that $3 \cdot -4 = -12$, it must also be true that $-4 \cdot 3 = -12$.

Ultimately, the reasoning expected of algebra students rests on a small set of laws about the operations, known as the Laws of Arithmetic[3] and assumed to be true. These laws are listed below.

For all numbers, *a*, *b*, and *c*:	
Commutative law of addition:	**Commutative law of multiplication:**
$a + b = b + a$ $5 + 9 = 9 + 5$	$ab = ba$ $3 \cdot 12 = 12 \cdot 3$
Associative law of addition:	**Associative law of multiplication:**
$(a + b) + c = a + (b + c)$ $(2 + 4) + 7 = 2 + (4 + 7)$	$(ab)c = a(bc)$ $(6 \cdot 2) \cdot 3 = 6 \cdot (2 \cdot 3)$
Distributive law of multiplication over addition:	
$(a + b)c = (ac) + (bc)$ $(3 + 2) \cdot 4 = (3 \cdot 4) + (2 \cdot 4)$	
Identity element for addition:	**Identity element for multiplication:**
$a + 0 = a$	$a \cdot 1 = a$
Inverse element for addition:	**Inverse element for multiplication:**
For every number *a*, there exists a number $-a$ such that $a + (-a) = 0$.	For every number *a* other than 0, there exists a number $1/a$ such that $a(1/a) = 1$.

As students work with these laws, they may develop new insights into the same generalizations they have explored through representations. For example, consider adding 1 to an addend versus adding 1 to a factor: Adding 1 to an addend can be written as $a + (b + 1) = (a + b) + 1$. This is an application of the associative law of addition. On the other hand, the rule for adding 1 to a factor can be written as $a(b + 1) = ab + a$, which is an application of the distributive law of multiplication over addition.

Secondary students who have had opportunities to explore the behavior of the operations in earlier grades will already be familiar with the content of the laws of arithmetic, for these very laws are among those generalizations they will have investigated.

IN CONCLUSION . . .

What kind of reasoning in the elementary grades prepares students to work with algebraic notation? They must be confident and fluent with the behavior of the operations, including the laws of arithmetic. Opportunities to explore these laws with numbers and representations prepare students to embrace and apply them later in symbolic form.

---

3 In this realm of formal proof, it is sufficient to specify the laws of addition and multiplication to be complete because $a - b$ is defined as $a + -b$ and $a \div b$ is defined as $a \times \frac{1}{b}$.

The middle school scenarios in this chapter show the importance of students working with representations to understand the meaning and behavior of the operations. Students like Joy and Joe have not thought about operations as entities with differing characteristics. This makes it difficult for them to work with algebraic expressions and equations in a meaningful way, and they tend to fall back on memorized procedures. In classrooms where students work with representations, the understanding of operations developed in earlier grades helps them compute with fractions and integers, recognize why and when algebraic expressions are equivalent, and interpret the process of solving equations.

Students must think about the operations as individual entities with their own sets of characteristics and relationships. They must recognize that

$$x + y = y + x$$

is a statement about addition, not about x and y. If students notice only numbers and letters when looking at an expression and barely register the operation symbols, they will not be able to succeed in algebra.

The kind of reasoning explored in this book is designed to develop rich and connected understanding of the behavior of the operations. This understanding will support students in their study of algebra. Students may no longer rely on representations for algebraic proofs, but it is the understanding developed through using these representations that allows students to move confidently into more abstract mathematical territory. In Chapter 10, we look at how such work can be integrated into the classroom over the course of a school year. ∎

LOOKING AHEAD TO THE MIDDLE GRADES

1. Chapter 9 focuses on middle school mathematics. What connections are there between the math content in the grade you teach and middle school mathematics?

2. As you read Chapter 9, you might have encountered mathematical ideas that you have not worked with for a while. What new mathematical thinking did Chapter 9 bring up for you? What math questions did it raise for you?

3. What connection did you note between:

    • whole-number computation and operating with fractions?

    • whole-number thinking and making sense of integers?

    • whole-number computation and multiplication with variables?

4. What is the role of representation in the excerpts on algebraic expressions and equivalent equations?

5. Consider your discussion of questions 3 and 4. In light of this discussion, what are the implications for your teaching of mathematics?

10
· · · · · · · · · · · ·

Building Across the School Year
Teachers and Students Learning Together

Developing a focus on generalization as part of the core computation curriculum can be new and unfamiliar territory. Yet this work is integral to learning about operations and is critical both for the mathematics students study in the elementary years and for later work in algebra.

Engaging all students in articulating, representing, and justifying general claims takes time and persistence. Regular routines designed to help students notice and describe behaviors of the operations are one way to begin. As students learn to notice and discuss regularities across sets of computation problems, generalization gradually becomes an everyday part of mathematics instruction. We now examine how this integration happens over a school year and revisit elements essential for this work: the establishment of a mathematics community that supports investigation of the operations and the consistent use of representations and story contexts.

GRADE 3: BUILDING A FOCUS ON OPERATIONS

Carolyn Michaels has been trying to integrate work on general claims into her third-grade class since the beginning of the school year. Although she noticed some sparks of ideas in the class conversations, she found that many students were not responding to the tasks and problems as she had envisioned. She was concerned about whether the way she orchestrated these discussions helped her students engage with their own ideas. In January, she wrote, "I am still a bit frustrated with our progress as a whole. My students have so many good ideas, but I am afraid that I am still leading them too much. Even though the thinking is there, the generalizations are not coming out the way I had hoped. I need to pay close attention to the tasks that I am asking of my students. I also want to give more time for representation and discussion among themselves."

As with many teachers just starting to integrate generalization into classroom work on number and operations, Ms. Michaels' progress was slow. The ideas were new to both her and her students. Unsure if students were beginning to think about how operations behave, she listened carefully to her students, keeping track of what they noticed, and looked for opportunities to work on general claims.

In February, students were generating subtraction expressions with a difference of 172. Ms. Michaels noticed that Laurine was systematically listing expressions in her math journal, starting with $192 - 20$, $193 - 21$, $194 - 22$, $195 - 23$, and continuing to $209 - 37$. Laurine was new to the math class and was struggling with much of the math work, so Ms. Michaels was very pleased to see Laurine engaged in generating this pattern. Though class was almost over, Ms. Michaels showed Laurine's work to the class and asked for comments. Students immediately began coming up with ideas, filling up the rest of class time. The next day Ms. Michaels begins discussion as follows:

⋯⋯⋯⋯⋯⋯⋯⋯⋯⋯⋯⋯⋯⋯⋯⋯⋯⋯⋯

Ms. Michaels: We talked about the pattern that was starting to develop. Does anyone remember what it was?

Chloe: Well, if you look at the 192 minus 20 equals 172, what she would do each time is she would add 1 to the 192 to make it 193. Then she would add 1 to the 20 so it would be 21. And it would keep adding and adding.

Ms. Michaels: I noticed when she did this, she would keep getting the difference of 172. I am wondering how that's working. Even though she kept changing the equation, how did she keep getting 172?

Shane: Um, after she started 1 number up, she subtracted 1 each time back. The first number was just going up adding 1 and while she was doing that her subtracting was subtracting on up. You know, taking 1 more away. And she kept getting 172 every time.

Kay: I think Shane is saying that she started with 1 number higher.

Dan: She added 1 up and then she subtracted 1 back. You know she had to take the 1 away that she added on . . . subtracting 1 more. You'll still be at the same number.

To make sure all students are making sense of the discussion, Ms. Michaels then models the students' claims with cubes and asks them to relate the cube model to the written equations.

Shane: I know, each time we add 1 on, we have to subtract the same 1 backwards. You have to take the original 1 off and the new ones you've added on.

Ms. Michaels notices that the students had progressed from a list of equations containing specific numbers to more general language. She asks them to try articulating a general claim.

Ms. Michaels: Can anyone state a rule that would always work?

William: When you're trying to get to a number and then you add 1, you have to add 1 to the number that you are subtracting from to get to the other number, you're going to have to subtract 1 more than you did before.

William tries to restate his rule more clearly:

William: When subtracting one number from another number to get to a certain number, if you add 1 more to the first number, then you have to subtract 1 more than before to end up with the same number.

Ms. Michaels records William's statement and asks students to work in pairs creating representations of this idea. Many use cubes, demonstrating that if 1 is added to the original amount, 1 more must be taken away to end up with the same difference.

After several students share their cube models, Dan and Oliver say they have something different to show. They had built a tower with 10 cubes, 4 red and 6 blue. They demonstrate 10 − 6 by removing the 6 blue cubes, leaving 4 red cubes. Then they reduce the total number of cubes to 9 (4 red and 5 blue), and show they would have to remove the 5 blue cubes to get the same difference.

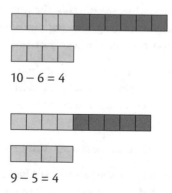

$$10 - 6 = 4$$

$$9 - 5 = 4$$

Dan: If I want to end up with the same number, I can only take away 5 this time. So if I take 1 away from the first number then I take 1 less away. That's different than what everybody else did, but I got the same answer.

Ms. Michaels wrote, "I had several children who wanted to go back to the statement that William had made about when you add 1 more on you have to take 1 more away. They were now convinced that you could also *take away* from the original model [the starting amount of the subtraction expression]. . . . I [also] had several students talking to their partners saying that they thought you could change the numbers by more than 1. It was very exciting. Most pairs were not only listening to each other, they were listening to the whole group, considering what everyone was saying."

Several key elements discussed in previous chapters are evident in these interactions:

1. *Noticing*: Ms. Michaels recognizes potentially important mathematics underlying Laurine's pattern, shows the class her work, and gives students time to analyze what is happening in the sequence of expressions.

2. *Math community*: Ms. Michaels makes key interventions during the discussion, pushing students to interact with each other to describe what they notice. She does not accept the first reasonable response she hears but asks for restatements and clarification, as she does following Chloe's contribution. She creates opportunities for students to participate in different ways—in whole-group discussion, in pairs, and through creating representations.

3. *Articulation*: Ms. Michaels recognizes when students are ready to attempt to articulate a general claim. She gives time for students to state and restate the claim. She recognizes that Dan and Oliver's idea could be used to expand the claim.

4. *Representation*: Ms. Michaels models the claim with cubes during the whole-group discussion and gives students time to create their own representations. As students do this, they focus on clarifying and expanding the ideas discussed in the whole group.

All of these elements took months to develop. During this time, Ms. Michaels reflected on her own practice. She paid close attention to how ideas about the behavior of the operations came up in students' work, and she persisted in asking students to investigate these ideas. By February, students are engaged seriously in thinking about the general behaviors of operations and how to state, represent, and prove a general claim.

Next we will focus on two of these key elements, establishing mathematics community and the use of representations, in two more classrooms. Toward the end of the chapter, we will revisit Ms. Michaels and her class.

GRADE 5: INCLUDING ALL STUDENTS IN THE MATHEMATICS COMMUNITY

In Chapter 2, we saw fifth-grade teacher Marlena Diaz building a math community in her classroom. She discussed explicitly with students how well math discussions were working, how to improve them, and how to identify and overcome obstacles that prevent students from participating fully. But having a discussion or two at the beginning of the year is not sufficient; focused work on engaging with each other's ideas about how the operations behave should continue throughout the year.

As her school year ended, Ms. Diaz wrote about nurturing these discussions in her classroom:

> The development of classroom community and discourse doesn't just happen. Both the students and I have to spend time explicitly reflecting and talking about our "math talking." Early in the year, we began to establish procedures for moving in and out of our horseshoe sitting arrangement, for turning and talking, and for the rephrasing and revoicing of ideas. We had to role-play, evaluate, and refine the way we talked and listened to each other. We had conversations about what to do when we were stuck or when we found ourselves "checking out" of a conversation. We discussed how wait time was being used in the whole-group discussions and in small-group discussions. These discussions helped the children become more aware of their role as part of a classroom community and allowed them to self-evaluate and to evaluate how they thought the class as a whole was progressing in creating an environment that supported learning. The class became better able to sustain long conversations over the course of the year. Small-group interactions were also impacted. Students were better able to navigate their own discussions, to compromise and justify ideas. I was also impressed how the range of learners in the classroom were able to find ways to enter and interact with these conversations—all students were challenged and pushed to improve their understanding of the operations and their strategies for computation.

One key component of building math community is ensuring that all students engage in the discussion. Whether students are struggling with grade-level computation or excelling at it, they cannot attain a deeper understanding of the behavior of the operations unless they grapple with the ideas. Every teacher faces students who fear failing or appearing "stupid" on the one hand, or believe they have nothing to learn on the other. In developing a math community, teachers need to address students with both these attitudes. Ms. Diaz writes about one of her learners, Lateia, who had not achieved grade-level benchmarks in mathematics the previous year:

> Early during the second semester of school, we had a conversation about how to acknowledge to yourself and to others when you were not following a line of thinking during a discussion. It was Lateia who modeled for the class how to be

responsible for one's own understanding. The day after we had the discussion about what do to when you are confused during a discussion, Lateia, who often had fragile understanding of mathematics concepts, stated, "I am confused about what is on the chart, about how n can be any number." She took a risk to make her confusion public, and she opened up the opportunity for others to also acknowledge confusions they were having. Lateia would often put her thumb up, ask for air time, and request that other students or myself rephrase an idea in order to help her get a hold on it. I was really proud of the manner in which she took control of, and responsibility for, her own learning. Her stance positively affected the other students. I am sure though that this would not have happened had we not established a community of respect and trust, one that valued learning opportunities embedded in confusions. This climate also positively affected the students' development of algebraic reasoning because they were able to push themselves into uncomfortable conversations, ones that expanded the ways that they viewed the operations or certain classes of numbers.

Students excelling in grade-level computation require support to help them understand how they can contribute to and benefit from math discussions. When discussing general claims, teachers often pose "easy" problems to keep the focus on the behavior of the operation, rather than on the computation. For this reason, some students who can do the computation with little effort may believe there is nothing else for them to learn (see, for example, Ms. Kaye's work with Trishna in Chapter 6).

Ms. Diaz attends to this entire range of students in class discussions. Will, for example, has a history of success in mathematics. Ms. Diaz describes him as "articulate, enthusiastic, and confident. His classmates respect him and look to him for guidance." Will is an active participant in mathematics discussions. Ms. Diaz writes that he "is quite eager to make observations and conjectures in 'rough draft' form. He often makes a quick observation, and in the same breath changes his mind and justifies his change of direction. He does not seem to be threatened when disagreeing with himself in front of his peers."

As the math community is established, students develop a sense of responsibility for each other's learning; they work to involve all students, regardless of their history of achievement. In a class conversation recounted by Ms. Diaz, Lateia and Will, as well as several other classmates, speak up:

⋯⋯⋯⋯⋯⋯⋯⋯⋯⋯⋯⋯⋯⋯⋯

Today, as we were finishing a discussion about fractions, and I was beginning to move to some work with equivalent expressions, an opportunity to "talk about our math talk" occurred. We have spent time as a class talking about how it feels to share your ideas in front of a group and to find yourself with nothing to say or totally mixed up. As Juan was in the midst of explaining what number corresponded to ⅓ of 24 on a number line, he stopped mid-sentence.

Juan: I am stuck. I don't know what I was thinking.

Ms. Diaz: If you are sharing an idea with the class and you find yourself sort of stuck, what do you do?

Juan: I try to go back and make a connection to something I know about. I also try to make a simpler problem.

Brent: I think about what the problem is about and then start over.

Lateia: Sometimes I go back to the beginning of the problem and revise what I was doing.

Eddie: Or you can keep your ideas and try some new ones you haven't come up with.

Will: I think you should think about the ideas that you said and what other possibilities there are that you haven't said.

Ms. Diaz: If you get stuck, could it feel embarrassing?

Keila: I don't worry about that any more because no one laughs.

Salena: Right, cause people listen and they say you are wrong but it is OK.

Ms. Diaz: That happened earlier today when we were having trouble following Brent's thinking about comparing ½ and ⅗. And lots of people asked questions and were interested in figuring out how his thinking could help us compare those fractions.

Setting the stage so that all students participate in generalization is key. Ms. Diaz explicitly shares responsibility with students for creating and maintaining a math community that values listening to and analyzing students' ideas.

GRADE 1: MAKING CONNECTIONS ACROSS REPRESENTATIONS

At the center of work on generalization is learning to make effective use of representations and story contexts. This capacity develops slowly over the course of the school year. Previous grades may have exposed students to representations and story contexts used only to demonstrate new concepts or as reinforcement for learners who were having difficulty. As teachers and students continue to build and use a repertoire of representations, they find them to be both tools for solving problems *and* images that allow deeper and more sophisticated investigations of mathematical ideas for all learners. When representation is consistently integrated into the arithmetic, students can fluently and frequently call on these images, choosing among them for the different insights they offer. For example, in Ms. Michael's class, Dan and Oliver used the cube model to help expand their claim about subtraction to include *decreasing* each number in the expression.

The use of connections among representations develops over time. Moving back and forth among different representations of an idea deepens and clarifies student understanding of the idea. Many teachers find that connecting story contexts to other representations is a powerful way to talk through the actions and behaviors of an operation. For example, connecting a multiplication context to a rectangular array or an addition context to a number line can illuminate how and why a generalization works in ways that a single representation may not. Even teachers quite experienced with representations of the operations have been surprised at the power of adding story contexts to their repertoire of drawings, models, and diagrams.

A *story context* is not the same as a *story problem*. A story context is an agreed-upon world of objects and actions. It is not simply a context for one particular problem involving one set of numbers; rather, it is a context that helps students visualize the behavior of an operation across problems using many different numbers. Story contexts effective for investigating general claims have several characteristics: they are familiar to students, so students can visualize the situation easily; they are simple enough that the action of the operation is easily discerned; and they are flexible, so that students can eventually use them to expand their claim to new classes of numbers, if appropriate.

Robert Williams' grade 1 class provides an example of how story contexts combine with other representations, helping students visualize regularities across multiple problems. Mr. Williams has introduced three representations students use to investigate equivalent addition expressions. The first is a story context about a car trip of a certain number of miles, where some number of miles has already been driven. For example, the trip's length might be 12 miles, with 3 miles driven, leaving 9 miles to go. The story context anchors the other two representations—cubes in two colors on a number board and a table.

1	2	3	4	5	6	7	8	9	10	11	12
▫	▫	▫	■	■	■	■	■	■	■	■	■

Miles driven	Miles to go	Total miles
1	11	12
2	10	12
3	9	12
4	8	12

By April, the students have become fluent with these connected representations. So far they have considered combinations of miles in a sequence, with the car gradually moving from the start to the end of the trip. For example, for a trip of 12 miles, they first consider 1 + 11 (1 mile driven, 11 miles to go), then 2 + 10 (2 miles driven, 10 miles to go), then 3 + 9, and so forth. Then Mr. Williams decides students are ready for a chart where miles driven and miles to go are not in sequence. He hopes this version will encourage students to think about why the expressions are all equivalent rather than rely only on the pattern of increasing and decreasing addends.

Miles driven	Miles to go	Total miles
3	9	12
6	6	12
1	11	12
5	7	12

···

Mr. Williams: What's happening to these numbers? I know many of you have talked about patterns. This time, I don't want to talk about the number patterns. I want to consider the changes occurring between the two groups of miles.

Peter: It's sort of because, um, when you drive 1, or when you drive 3 miles, you still don't have like 12 to go. Because you already drove 3, you need to take away 3 since you've already driven them.

Mr. Williams: Where are you taking the 3 away from?

Peter: From the 12.

Mr. Williams: What is happening to the miles to go number?

Robert: It's getting smaller. Umm, you're taking 1 from every, each number, you're taking it away and you're adding that number to the miles driven. And the miles driven is getting higher and higher and higher.

Mr. Williams: Tell me some more about that.

Robert: So the miles to go, so you are taking away one number from the miles to go and adding it up onto the other number, um, miles driven. Then the miles driven is, um, 1 mile higher.

Mr. Williams: Who can explain what Robert is talking about?

Al: Every time you drive a mile, the other miles are getting, are going away. Like this *[demonstrating with the cubes on the number board]*—you drove 2 more miles and those miles went away.

Japesh: Every time you drive more miles, the miles to go gets less.

Mr. Williams: How much less does it change?

Japesh *[after some silence]*: When you drive 3 miles, the miles to go gets less by 3.

Mr. Williams: What would happen if you drove 5 miles?

Japesh: The miles to go would get less by 5.

Mr. Williams: Is it the same each time? Does it change by the same amount? What do we think about that?

Mary *[again, after some silence]*: Like in the first time when you drove 3 miles, 3 less than 12 is 9 so it went down 3. And then, when you drove 3 more miles, 3 less than 9 is 6. So it was 6.

Elizabeth: Since when you drive 3 miles, the miles to go is 3 less since you're driving that much miles.

After class Mr. Williams wrote:

The class is beginning to talk more abstractly about the changing addends. By questioning my students and engaging them in a group share, the children have begun to shift their focus from the specific problems and numbers to talking more generally about the changes to both addends. Many of the children are speaking about the relationship between these addends. I think the experience of enacting a story context with quantities of cubes and recording the changing quantities on a chart is leading to a heightened awareness of this inverse relationship.

First graders frequently refer to specific numbers in their explanations. However, Mr. Williams noticed that, although their investigation might involve specific numbers, their intention was often to describe the behavior of operations for any numbers (or, at least, any numbers familiar to first graders). Over time, they began to summarize their discoveries in more general language. For example, one student summarized the previous discussion this way: "The numbers are changing because when you drive a mile, the miles to go get smaller by how much you drive. It would work with any number." The image of the car trip became one that many referred to. A few weeks later, Mr. Williams works with Yvette, one of his students who struggles with grade-level computation. Yvette has been working with another student, Catherine, on equivalent addition expressions.

....

Mr. Williams: Can you make 7 plus 10 into 6 plus 11?

Catherine: Yes, I think you can because taking 1 away from the 7 and adding it to the, like, I take 1 away from the 7 and it's 6 and I add that 1 to the 10 to make 11.

Yvette: 1 goes, ahh, I know what it reminds me of.

Mr. Williams: What's that?

Yvette: Those charts. Because one side going down and the other side. It's like "miles driven" and "miles to go."

....

Stories aren't just for students in the primary grades. Stories can be used as representations for math learning at any age. For older students, a story context provides an image of relationships between expressions and allows students to picture what happens when a value in the expression changes. Ms. Kaye's third graders use the context of jewelry boxes to understand the result of adding 1 to a factor in a multiplication expression (Chapter 8), and Ms. McLeod's seventh graders visualize hammocks 4 feet longer than the height of the person to represent the expression $x + 4$ (Chapter 9).

Before using a particular representation to justify a general claim about an operation, students must become familiar with how it represents that operation. For example, students have to understand how rectangular arrays represent the factors and products in multiplication equations before using them to investigate the effect of doubling one factor. Students also need experience using a story context to solve problems before using it to examine and prove general claims. Fluency with representations such as story contexts is key to development of the mental images students need to expand their understanding of the operations, articulate general claims, and create arguments for why their claims must be true.

REFLECTING ON ONE'S OWN PRACTICE

As teachers persistently ask questions and pose problems about the operations over the school year, both teacher and students become more attuned to the investigation of general claims. Let's return to Ms. Michaels, whose class we visited in February at the beginning of this chapter. It is the first year in which she has attempted to integrate work on the behavior of the operations into her curriculum. As part of a professional development project, she has periodically tape-recorded her classes and used the recordings to reflect on her practice. Here is an excerpt from her reflection during the final weeks of school:

What did I accomplish this year? Talking about general claims or generalizations in math was somewhat new to me. At the beginning of the year, I felt like many of the conversations we had were forced. As I listened to my recordings, I found myself asking leading questions. I took that as an opportunity to grow as a facilitator. Listening to yourself teach is eye-opening. There have been mixed emotions as I have listened to my recordings:

- *Amazement—as I listen to my students listen to one another restating their ideas*

- *Frustration—when the children just wouldn't think about what I thought they would or should*

- *Disappointment—when I realize that I missed a great opportunity to ask the perfect question*

- *Enjoyment—as I walked around the room and witnessed students who were completely engaged in trying to prove an idea they had*

- *Regret—when that moment was missed to push that student to the next level*

- *Surprise—as students started to question mathematical ideas on their own when I was not asking the questions*

As I listened to our classroom discussions sitting in my cozy chair in my living room on Saturday mornings, I began to think about what I could do differently. . . . I have put more thought into what we need to work on next. I have put more thought into how I can bring these mathematical discussions into my regular math instruction rather than planning a separate "talk" like I did in the beginning. All this thought about the importance of reflecting [for myself] made me think about how I wasn't asking my students to reflect on their thinking. . . . By the end of the year, I didn't have to ask for specific points to be made. Students were making mathematical connections all on their own. They were grappling with ideas about how operations act differently and how even and odd numbers affect changes in sums, differences, and products. . . . This was a difficult group of children as a whole, and they made great strides in their ability to reflect in a short period of time. I can't wait to put these ideas into practice at the beginning of the year next year.

Over the year, Ms. Michaels developed the practice of reflecting on both her students' work and her own actions, interventions, and words. Her students were not able to respond to her questions at first, but she persisted in bringing their attention to the behavior of the operations. She asked them what they noticed and why it was happening. Gradually, students started addressing these questions without being asked. Her remarks bring us back to the first two chapters of this book: Ms. Michaels *noticed* generalizations that came up in her students' arithmetic, persisted in *helping students learn to share what they noticed* about consistencies across problems, and *planned regular opportunities* to investigate, articulate, represent, and justify generalizations about these consistencies. With one year of experience behind her, she has more confidence and skill to engage next year's students in these ideas.

THREE PILLARS OF NUMBER AND OPERATIONS

At the heart of mathematics is posing one's own questions about mathematical relationships. To truly engage in mathematics is to become curious and intrigued about regularities and patterns, then describe and explain them. As mathematician Lynn Steen writes in *On the Shoulders of Giants*, "Seeing and revealing hidden patterns are what mathematicians do best" (1990, 1). A focus on the behavior of the operations allows students starting in the familiar territory of number and computation to progress to true engagement in the discipline of mathematics. By looking across problems, they formulate and investigate conjectures. As they pursue such questions, they discover their own curiosity about mathematics. As Steen goes on to say, "By encouraging students to explore patterns that have proven their power and significance, we offer them broad shoulders from which they will see farther than we can" (8).

In the elementary grades, the study of arithmetic is central to the curriculum. Deep understanding of this territory rests on three pillars: understanding numbers, developing computational fluency, and examining the behavior of the operations:

- *Understanding numbers* includes understanding written and oral counting, the structure of the base ten system with whole numbers and decimals, the meaning of fractions, and the meaning of zero and of quantities less than zero.

- *Developing computational fluency* includes building a repertoire of accurate, efficient, and flexible strategies for each operation and knowing how and when to apply them.

- *Examining the behavior of the operations* includes modeling these operations, recognizing contexts in which each applies, learning about the unique set of properties of each operation, describing and justifying behaviors that are consequences of those properties, and comparing and contrasting the behaviors of different operations.

IN CONCLUSION . . .

The third pillar of number and operations is as crucial as the others. It is not additional content but a way of thinking about the mathematics that underlies both arithmetic and algebra. Making generalizations about how operations behave is an essential mathematical activity. Generalizing about the operations is not about particular answers but about the operations themselves as important objects of study. The properties of the operations, and behaviors based on those properties, underlie all computation strategies. Noticing, articulating, representing, and justifying these properties and behaviors engage and support all students' mathematical work in the elementary grades and provide crucial links to their future study of algebra. ■

REFERENCE

Steen, Lynn Arthur. 1990. "Pattern." In *On the Shoulders of Giants: New Approaches to Numeracy*, edited by L. A. Steen. Washington, DC: National Academy of Sciences.

FOCUS QUESTIONS

BUILDING ACROSS THE SCHOOL YEAR: TEACHERS AND STUDENTS LEARNING TOGETHER

1. Chapter 10 offers images of students and teachers working on representing general claims as a year-long endeavor. The first excerpt, the case of Ms. Michaels, includes a list of four aspects of her work with students: Noticing, Math Community, Articulation, and Representation. After reading this book, what does each of these terms mean to you? In what ways do you plan to include these elements in your own teaching?

2. In the next excerpt, Ms. Diaz shares how developing a math community requires year-long attention and how she explicitly brings her students into analyzing how math discussions can work for them. What is your reaction to her comments? What aspects of this work do you plan to incorporate into your own teaching? How?

3. In the course of reading this book, how have your ideas about story contexts and other representations evolved?

4. The chapter concludes with a description of the "three pillars of number and operations." What is your reaction to the description of these three pillars? How does that fit with your own thinking about math instruction? What questions are you still left with?

INDEX
. . . .

A
Addition
adding 1 to a factor, 120–23
adding 1 to an addend, 103, 117–19
distinguishing between operations, 48, 92–95, 123
equivalent expressions, 39–41, 62–63, 76–80, 83–84, 100
ideas about addition, articulating, 39–42, 47–48
identifying addition expressions, 100–102
laws of arithmetic, 144–45
relationship to subtraction, 25–28
Algebraic expressions, creating images for, 140–41
Algebraic notation
arithmetic symbols, making meaning for, 90–99
choosing when to address issues of notation, 97–99
issues in using, 106–8
letters are not always variables, 107–8
making meaning for, 89–90, 100–10

not all generalizations can be represented by, 106–7
problems with learning, students', 89–90
using variables to express a generalization, 100–4, 119, 122
x is sometimes less than 0, 108
Arithmetic symbols
choosing when to address issues of notation, 97–99
connecting actions to equations, 90–92
distinguishing between different operations, 92–95
interpreting the equal sign, 95–97
making meaning for, 90–99

C
Computation
connections, looking for, 82–85
difficulty with grade-level, 68–78
excelling in grade-level, 78–85
finding patterns in, 78–80
fluency, developing, 160